OnTheRoadWith
BLUE

Blue is managed by Daniel Glatman for Intelligent Music Management Ltd.

First published in 2003 by Contender Books
48 Margaret Street
London
W1W 8SE

www.contendergroup.com

This edition published 2003

1 3 5 7 9 10 8 6 4 2

ISBN 1 84357 091 2

Typesetting by E-Type
Cover designed by Button One-to-One
Plate sections designed by designsection, Frome, Somerset
Repro by Radstock Repro, Midsomer Norton, Bath
Printed and bound in Great Britain by Butler & Tanner Ltd, Frome and London
Production: Sasha Morton

Front cover image: Max Dodson / Virgin Records Ltd
Pictures supplied by: Virgin International, All-Action Pictures, PA Photos,
Rex Features, Kyran O'Brien, Wattie Cheung, Blue Official Fanclub
Pg 4 David Tonge / TV Hits Magazine / Idols Licensing and Publicity Ltd
Pg 8 Bellak / Dalle / Idols Licensing and Publicity Ltd
Pg 1, 2, 3 Fryderyk Gabowicz / Idols Licensing and Publicity Ltd
Pg 2, 3, 4, 6, 7 Sam Jones / Popworld Magazine / Idols Licensing and Publicity Ltd

OnTheRoadWith

BLUE

CONTENTS

REHEARSING THE TOUR: PART ONE

chapter one

6PM ON A WEDNESDAY evening, sometime in October 2003. It's cold, and it's raining, but in a warehouse room somewhere on an industrial trading estate in the wilds of south London, Antony Costa, Lee Ryan, Duncan James and Simon Webbe are dripping with sweat. Sprawled on a sofa and panting heavily, Simon reaches for a bottle of water and glugs half of it down. He wipes his brow and turns to Duncan. "You know what, Dunc? This is going to be an amazing tour."

Blue have been holed up in the Music Bank rehearsal space for the past week, and they're due to be here for at least another seven days. Or, at least, as long as it takes to get the live show right. In a month from now the band will be hitting the road on a punishing UK tour; their biggest yet and the one, they hope, which will establish them as the country's premier live group. It's not a challenge they're taking lightly – there's the blood, sweat, blisters and late nights to prove it – and right now every ounce of these four lads' energy is going into this tour.

On the table in front of Blue are dozens of pieces of paper. On each of them is a Blue song title, from 'All Rise' right through to the tracks on the band's new album. It's like their entire career flashing before their eyes. The pieces of paper are in some sort of order, though each of the lads keeps pushing the songs into different parts of the table. With towels round their necks, Blue sit in silence. They're sorting out the tour set list, and there's a whole new album's worth of songs to take into account. But figuring out where they should fit into the concert is a tricky business. The set list is the most important element in the planning of a new show, the entire performance is built around it, so it's vital that they make the right decisions in order to make the show as good as it possibly can be.

"I like all these songs," declares Ant, but at the same time he knows they unfortunately can't be on stage for three and a half hours.

The lads discuss Madonna, whose last tour totally rewrote her musical history to suggest that she'd always been as cool as she currently perceives herself as being.

"I think a lot of artists try to do that," Duncan adds. "They try to get away from who they really are. At the end of the day the people who are buying our tickets want to see all the hits they've bought. They want to have a boogie and sing along to the words. We always want to make sure our fans get to have a good singalong."

At this point in their career, many bands wouldn't be too bothered about their set lists. After all, tickets for the tour sold out months ago. But the lads know it's their reputation which has sold those tickets, and not only do they intend to live up to that reputation, they're hoping to build it up even further.

"OK," Ant decides. "So let's say we're doing 15

songs. We're going to do all the singles, which is seven. And maybe four new tracks from the new album. That means we can only do two tracks from each of our first two albums."

It is, the boys realise, going to be really difficult to select the remaining songs. Feeling in the Blue camp is that even on the last album, *One Love*, there were four more songs which could easily have been singles. So the boys take a slightly different approach to the set list. Because they'll be singing live, they'll need to pace the set so that they can catch their breath at key points in the show. This is where the ballads come in. They start shifting the paper around again, this time to include ballads every few songs. "Thing is," Ant says, "while we do release the odd ballad, we're not really a ballad band, are we?"

It's clearly going to be a long process, and the band decide that they need to come back to the task with a clear head. With the rehearsal studio booked late into the night, Blue have got time to grab some food in a nearby restaurant, so they put books and mugs on the pieces of paper to keep them all in order and decamp to an Italian round the corner.

As we wait for food to arrive, the set list is still playing on Duncan's mind. "Before we did our first ever tour," he explains, "I remember we were in Germany and a set list was faxed through to the hotel. The production company had put it together and when we looked at it we were, like, 'What? We're not doing THAT!' We wrote out our own set list, and faxed it back. Since then we've always worked on set lists from scratch." The waitress appears with wine, and Dunc gets back to chatting with the lads.

There's someone else at the table, too. You'll be reading a lot about him in this book. He's not a member of Blue, but at the same time Blue wouldn't work without him. Meet Johnny B, the shaven-headed man mountain whose job description is Tour Manager. In reality, this means a lot more. He's Jack of all trades, master of every single one. "Basically," he says, "I'm mum. If there's a problem, mum sorts it out. Whether it's a problem with a gig, or a photo shoot, or a headache, or anything, I sort it out."

At 45 (which by his own admission makes him "an old git"), Johnny's been around the music industry for over two decades. He's seen the pop superstars come and go, and one of the first bands he saw come (and then go) were eighties pop idols Bros – two brothers called Matt and Luke Goss and their mate, Craig Logan. These days the three members are still working in and around the entertainment industry (Matt's just relaunched his pop career, Luke's an actor and Craig manages the likes of Pink and Triple 8), but at their popstar peak the trio were massive as massive can be.

"Working with Bros was a very good initiation into the music business," Johnny says, smiling. "I was 28 when their manager, Tom Watkins, pulled me in to work with them as their security. It was a mad few years: the first time I went out on the road with them I was told to pack a bag for a week. I eventually went home three months later."

Pop was a different place in the late eighties. In 2003 there are more bands than there are fans to go around, but at that point Bros were *the* pop band. Imagine if, today, Blue had all their fans – plus all Westlife's fans, plus all Justin's fans, plus every other pop fan in the UK, and you might have some idea how chaotic life on the road was. Johnny was looking after the three members, by himself, for 18 months.

During the nineties, Johnny worked with another of Tom Watkins's bands – East 17 – for six and a half years. Throughout the history of pop, there've always been bands who bounce off each other: in the sixties the Beatles and the Rolling Stones were the first example of a clean-cut boyband (the Beatles) and their more rough-edged, laddy rivals (the Stones). In today's charts you can see the same thing with Westlife and Blue, and in the nineties, there were Take That and East 17. Take That were the shiny, highly choreographed disco kids and East 17, four lads from the east London borough of Walthamstow, were the rough boys. The band eventually imploded, after which Johnny worked with All Saints, and then with Victoria and David Beckham when Posh was promoting her solo singles. During one of Beckham's public appearances Johnny B met Blue's manager, Daniel Glatman, backstage, and a working relationship was born. He was introduced to the new band a few weeks later.

His first impression? "Very young," Johnny laughs. "Very young." He explains that the first few weeks with a band are massively important in terms of nurturing trust, understanding and the basis of a good working relationship – as he points out, the band could flop, or the tour manager could be rubbish, and everyone has to know where they stand. "It's all about trust," he says, "and if there's no trust, it won't work."

The band are full of respect for Johnny B. "He works even harder than we do," Simon says. "He's up before we are and goes to bed last. I've got the utmost respect for him. *Utmost* respect." He leans over the table and drops his voice to a whisper. "He's good at airports, too. I think a lot of women behind the counter actually fancy him, so we get good seats. And I see how all the fans' mums look at him. They go, 'Ooooh, Johnny!'" Simon guffaws.

While we continue to wait for food to arrive, Blue reflect on their year to date. Though they haven't had an album out yet in 2003, it's impossible for a band like Blue to be out of the public eye, and many events have taken place in the run-up to this tour.

The boys agree that one of the high points of the year was an appearance, early in the summer, at the closing ceremony of the 2003 Special Olympics. This time round the Special Olympics were held in Dublin, and the band led something of a stage invasion during their set.

Simon laughs. "The security guys were going mental, going, 'No! Don't let the audience on stage! And I was just going, 'C'mon, look how happy everyone is. What are they going to do? Beat us up?'"

"I enjoyed that *so* much," Lee adds. "Dragging all

those kids up on stage was such an exhilarating feeling. That was one of the most amazing things. I came off stage on such a buzz that night. That sort of event really affirms my faith in the human spirit. It makes you think, though – these people have so much love to give and yet there are people who don't have any time for them. In schools, in society at large. People don't learn to live with things, they make people feel inadequate and sometimes sweep them under the carpet."

The world, Lee feels, would change if people just listened to other people. "If I could change one thing in the world," he says, "it would be how we teach kids. If you teach kids how to love instead of how to hate – being competitive all the time – then the world would be so different." Being dyslexic, Lee himself has experience of this. At school he was always put to the back of the class, and told that he would amount to nothing. "When people are told that, it totally wrecks their lives. Any personality or creativity is just dragged out of people. The Special Olympics are great, though – difference is celebrated."

Simon agrees. "We ran on stage and it was like 65 countries in one place and that was just like my dream – all the world coming together. Doing that show totally overrides any bad press we've had this year. It makes you realise that none of it matters. Our music was louder than the newsprint, know what I'm saying?"

Simon's had plenty on his mind this year, in the few spare days when he hasn't been seeing to Blue business. One of his projects is a new band called VS – an urban boy/girl band he's managing. In the early days of 2003 the band signed to Blue's label, Innocent, but the process wasn't quite as easy as that makes it sound. It is, in fact, quite a long story, so as he munches on his salad starter Simon runs us through an abridged version.

"The whole thing stems back four or five years, when I was at an audition for a band. I didn't get in and the woman who was running it told me something I'll never forget: 'Hip hop and R&B will never break through in the British pop charts'. I knew she'd be wrong, and the charts today are all the proof you need. I've always liked the idea of a hip hop group who are presented in the pop arena, so it's something I've had in the back of my mind since then. Anyway, one day I was at my record label and I noticed that they'd signed this girl I'd been championing for ages for a development deal. I thought to myself, 'Well, if I've been right about her being the right stuff, perhaps I've really got an eye for this thing'."

Shortly afterwards, one of Simon's mates was putting together a band of his own, and Simon said he'd help out by pointing some talented kids he knew in the direction of his mate's audition. "I knew what I was looking for, and at the same time I couldn't put my finger on it," he recalls. "It's that X factor, innit? You can have the best voice in the world but if you ain't got the X factor, you can forget it. So I sent along people that I thought had the X factor." Simon was surprised when none of the people he'd put forward got into the group. "So I decided, 'Bollocks to this, I'll do it myself'."

Which is what he did. Once the five members were

in place, Simon took a demo to his label boss, Hugh Goldsmith, at Innocent. When the songs had finished, Goldsmith told Simon: "If they look as good as they sound, you've got a deal for your band." Simon says that he laughed. "I said, 'Are you *sure* you want to say that?' And he's like, 'Er, yeah'. The deal was signed that week."

As we chat, VS are currently in development at Innocent – that lengthy period between signing a deal and unleashing yourself on the world of pop. Simon has high hopes for the band. "I've invested a lot in this act," he says. "I wouldn't have done that if I didn't think they'd make it. I'm a strong believer that if you're in a position to help somebody else and you can, then you should."

Si picks his CD Walkman out of his coat and rustles around in the bottom of his bag, eventually producing a CD-R. On the front is scrawled, in red marker pen, 'VS tracks'. He clicks it into the CD player and offers his headphones. To be fair, the tracks are pretty impressive

– fully rounded soundscapes with an irresistible urban edge, and reference points ranging from old-school hip hop to modern artists like NERD. One of the songs, Simon explains, is about girls that go for older guys when really they should be going for guys their own age. VS isn't the extent of Simon's entrepreneurship, either. Since buying shares in his old modelling agency, the agency has become Manchester's most popular, and there's another act sitting alongside VS in Simon's music production company, Love 4 Music. This time it's a solo artist called Blarney whose material Simon is hoping to feed out into the clubs next spring.

Lee, too, has been working on projects outside of Blue. One of his most high profile moments came with the song 'Stand Up As People', which Lee wrote in response to the worsening global political climate, and which was subsequently adopted by many teenagers as a peace anthem when war broke out in the spring. At that point the song was added to *Hope*, a compilation album which had been put together by the War Child charity, and Lee found himself on *CD:UK*, on his own for the very first time.

"Being up there on stage by myself, doing a live vocal, was weird," he admits. "In fact I was really nervous. It was scary." He pauses for a short while. "It's strange – in spite of all that, the song didn't end up getting that much coverage, and I'm still not sure whether the record company wanted me to do it. I can see that there might have been a bit of a stigma around a 'solo' song in case people thought I was going to split the band up or something, but it's a shame. For me I think it went beyond the fact that it was Lee Ryan's time to shine as a solo artist, because it wasn't about that. It was about the lyrics. I wouldn't even have cared if someone else had sung it, just as long as people were hearing the words."

You certainly can't say Lee didn't work at getting the song out there. He took it to radio himself (it later became one of Capital FM's most requested songs), and recalls the struggle he had to be taken seriously when he first had the idea. "I said to Hugh at Innocent, 'I'm going to get Christina Aguilera, Justin Timberlake, Elton John', all these names. He said to me: 'If you get these names, I'll do everything I can for you'. So the next week I was in LA having dinner and I looked across the restaurant. There, sitting with a friend, was Justin Timberlake."

Lee plucked up all his courage and went over to Justin. With a slight bending of the truth he told Justin that he'd *already* done a song with Elton John and explained the motives for the single – that the money would go to kids, that it'd create awareness of the fact that in war the biggest losers are future generations. Justin didn't seem very interested: he shrugged his shoulders and carried on talking with his friend.

"So I walked off," Lee recalls. "And as I was walking back to my table, I thought, 'Why doesn't he care?' So I walked back to Justin's table. And as I started to talk to him, he turned his back on me. So I grabbed his shoulder, spun him around and went, 'Look, I'll be in touch with you in two weeks. You don't have to do anything. Just wait for me to get in touch'."

Two weeks later, to the day, Blue were recording a TV show in Italy and by coincidence the crew wanted to film the band giving a message to another celebrity. To Justin Timberlake. Lee's message? "Awright, Justin? Remember me? I told you I'd get in touch! How about this charity song, then?" When the TV show played the video back to Justin, live on air, he was full of praise for Lee, agreeing to call and hook up for a recording session. In the end, though, Justin didn't bother.

"I found the whole process so frustrating," Lee remembers. "I was asking all sorts of people, from Christina to Coldplay. Coldplay just looked at me like I was an idiot. Nobody seemed to understand that I wasn't doing it for my own personal publicity: I was doing it because it was the way I could do something for children who didn't have *anything*. It would literally have been an hour's work for anyone involved."

In the end, Lee recorded the song himself, but even

then there was abuse in store. George Michael – once a teen popster himself – came along and dissed the track, saying that Lee, being so young, had no experience in life and therefore no authority to record a war song. (He later apologised to Lee in person.) "I just think that with things like that you have to keep plugging away," Lee shrugs. "I guess it's a work ethic I got from my mum. Without my dad at home, she could quite easily have sat on her arse and gone, 'Right, I'll just collect my child support and do no work'. But that didn't even cross her mind – she went out, and she worked. She worked *hard*. I've got that same ethic. I don't give up easily."

Someone who the band discovered wasn't quite prepared to go that extra mile – at least on the day when they were supposed to meet her – was Madonna. During the spring the lads had been booked on to a French TV show in which various acts each covered Madonna hits in the presence of Madge herself. Blue covered 'Like A Prayer' – one of her biggest, and most controversial hits.

"She refused to meet us," Ant huffs as he tucks into his main course of chicken and veg. "And I have no idea why. In fact we weren't even allowed to listen to the soundcheck she did for her *own* performance."

"It was a bit disappointing," Simon admits with a shake of the head. "I think when you're a celebrity and you've got another celebrity travelling overseas to sing one of your songs on a show which is a tribute to *you*... Well, I'd like to think I'd stick around and at least say 'Hi'. Maybe you'd even stick your head around the dressing room door and say 'Thanks'. She didn't even bother to send one of her skivvies round to say hello. We did sit there wondering, 'Well, why are we bothering?'."

None of the boys own a recording of their 'Like A Prayer' cover and nobody seems very bothered about ever hearing it again: it seems the experience was a rather negative one, and you get the impression that the cover might not actually have been much cop, though none of them says as much. How, one wonders, will

Blue stop themselves turning into the kind of celebrities they hate?

"I'd like to think we're grounded people," Simon says. "And I also know that everyone around us will keep us grounded, too. Which is really important with all the mad stuff that's happening around us."

One example of mad stuff is the fact that at the beginning of 2003 Blue won their second Brit Award. Their appearance at the Brits was especially notable because, for the first time, Simon's hair was unleashed as a full-blown afro. He laughs at the effect his new hairstyle had on people. "I've always wanted to wear my hair out but it's always been a thing of 'Ooh, you look a bit scary with an afro'. Still, for the Brits, Maarit, who does our hair and make-up, and Caroline, who's our stylist, both agreed that I should take my braids out. To begin with I was reluctant but everybody else in the band was, like, 'C'mon, Si, get your hair out!' so I didn't have much choice in the matter!"

During the show, Blue performed their *One Love*

album track, 'Riders', with 20 dancers. The song – which has a much harder edge than any of their singles – had proved a good show opener on the previous year's arena tour, and it went down a storm at the Brits, too. But when it came to the award for Best Pop Act, the boys didn't think they'd won.

"When we won the Best Newcomer award the year before, the TV cameras were all positioned by our table when the results were being read out," Simon explains. "But this year the cameras were all over by Gareth Gates, so we assumed we'd lost to him. We were all preparing our 'We're really happy for the person who's won even though it's not us' faces, when suddenly they read our name out, and all these cameras just appeared at our table from out of nowhere, man! On the way up to collect the award my pants fell down because I had no belt on, Lee and Duncan were jumping on each other's backs, it was just crazy. Crazy but brilliant."

Crazy but brilliant: a pretty good summary of Blue's year. They pay their restaurant bill and make their way back to the rehearsal studio, hoping to sort out once and for all what their tour set list might look like. They're limbering up to get back on the road but, really, they've been on the road for the past six months, crossing continents, meeting friends old and new, doing everything you do when you're in Blue. It's been an exhausting summer, so let's rewind a few months and start our story five miles away from the wet concrete of this south London rehearsal studio...

ON THE ROAD

chapter two

WE'RE IN LONDON'S Hyde Park, on 6 July 2003. The sun beats down on an expanse of greenery right in the middle of London so big that, even with six miles of fencing sectioning off an area big enough for 100,000 people, there's still miles of field all around it.

To say that Party In The Park is a big deal is a bit like calling Blue 'quite popular'. It's the largest one-day pop event in Europe and, over the past six years, has become *the* summer pop event for London town, bringing in music fans from infants to the elderly and everywhere between. This year, tickets have sold out in record time (an impressive feat, considering that last year all 100,000 tickets went in just under five hours), and hopes are high that it'll be the best Party In The Park ever.

Preparing the site has been a massive operation. As the Blue entourage drives through the backstage gates we find hundreds of vans, workers, tents and stalls. Even backstage there are 120 different Portakabins – some are dressing rooms, others are security rooms, others are 'operation rooms' where walkie talkies buzz through the day and all manner of crises are ironed out to make sure the whole thing runs smoothly. Security is at a premium – there are 640 security staff patrolling the site, and not just for the benefit of the popstars, because the cost of replacing a damaged tree in Hyde Park is a whopping £10,000.

The whole backstage area is dripping with fame and celebrity – and there are TV crews and pop reporters here too, their mission being to grab a minute with as many stars as possible. Indeed, as pop's biggest names circle the backstage enclosure in golf buggies, people-carriers and blacked-out limos, nobody would ever guess that the site was once a hunting ground for King Henry VIII, or that if we were stood here during World War II, we'd have our feet right in the middle of a turnip allotment.

We're shown to Blue's dressing room for the day. The boys are here for two reasons: firstly, all four of them will be appearing on stage at the end of the day, performing five songs to the frenzied (and probably by that point a little sunburned) crowd. Duncan has another duty, too: he'll be co-presenting live coverage of the event on Channel 5, from the moment the show goes on air right up to the minute he goes out on stage. The dressing room is standard fare for this sort of event, and Caroline Watson, the band's stylist since 'Too Close', is already here getting the boys' stage outfits ready for the afternoon's performance.

While Simon rummages his way through her oversized wheely suitcase, Caroline explains the circumstances of her first meeting with Simon, and it seems she met him just in time. Picture it: London,

1998… the black magazine *Pride* was holding its annual model search for the face of the year. Twelve guys and twelve girls had made it down to the final and Caroline was booked to make sure that they looked their best for the catwalk section. In most cases, the clothes the aspiring models brought along were perfect for the show and Caroline had no need to make any alterations. But then there was Simon. He was tall, Caroline noticed. And he was pretty gorgeous. But the first thing she noticed was what the wannabe model was wearing.

"Unfortunately," Caroline splutters, "Simon didn't have any taste." Simon was wearing what he later revealed was his 'pulling shirt'. In reality the shirt was "really cheap-looking, a sort of satin-effect Polyester number which looked like he'd bought it in an everything-five-quid shop on Oxford Street". Caroline vowed that there was no way she'd allow this hopeful on to the catwalk in the world's worst shirt. Simon seemed offended at first but she offered him a deal: "Try on this suit, and you'll win."

He went out on the catwalk and, in Caroline's own words, "He only went and won the bloody thing, didn't he?" From that point onwards she'd bump into Simon in clubs and bars every now and again, then one day opened a magazine to find his face staring back. "I remember thinking, 'Aw, good on him – he's got himself a modelling contract'," Caroline recalls, "because he was stood there looking really good with three other guys." Except the magazine article was actually one of Blue's first ever interviews and when, a few weeks later, some guy on the other end of the phone introduced himself with, "Hi Caroline, how many black guys do you know from Manchester?", she knew that it was Simon; fate had brought them together once again. She's been working with the lads ever since. "They're like my brothers now," she grins. "I can't do without them, they can't do without me. I've got the role of big sister. When they're in a sleepy or grumpy mood, I'm the one who tries to get them up or tries and get them hyped up. I'm like, 'Come on, boys, we can do this!'."

Lee's sitting at the table with a pen in his hand. Spread open in front of him is an A4-size, black, leather-bound book. It's about an inch thick; on the front, in gold lettering, is printed '*Book Of Shadows*'. "This," he says, "is a special book."

Indeed it is. For as long as he can remember, Lee's been writing poetry and odd little verses in books just like this. This particular book, about two thirds full, represents his work for the last year or so – a turbulent 12 months whose twists and turns are all included here. "I don't show this book to many people," he whispers, and as he flicks through the pages, it's easy to see why. Every page is a window into Lee's mind. That's the *real* Lee Ryan – the private and sensitive Lee Ryan whose thoughts and opinions are all here, scribbled down in hotel rooms, tour buses, departure lounges and dressing rooms in every corner of the world. Some of the pages contain little more than poetic doodles, others boast fully formed poems. Right now he's searching for one particular poem. It doesn't have a name, but when he eventually finds it, he begins to read it out loud.

> God created man through the image of himself
> He took the creation of life and made this monster for
>   all living things
> He had his skies as his painting brush and his tears
>   as the watercolours
> And He said: I created these to destroy me, so he
>   gave us hands
> And He said: I give you eyes for you to close, not to see,
>   so he gave us sight
> He then said: I give you truth for you to know dishonesty
> The last thing God said was I created man but man
>   created me.

Lee explains that the poem came from his confusion about the existence of God. "The idea is that God created us," he says. "But if you look around, the only thing which could really have created us is the planet. So I believe that God is the planet – if you look under every rock He's there. That seems a lot more likely than some bloke standing around with a bit of putty and

Plasticine. I don't believe God's a man standing there with a beard, standing like that, going, 'Oh yes, oh yes' all the time. He's not. He's bigger than that. He's inside us, and around us... and we just destroy the planet, and him, every day we're alive."

Lee gets up and wanders around the room looking for his phone, but continues talking. "I guess I'm more spiritual than religious. A people who really inspire me are the Native American Indians. Their quotes and their philosophies are amazing. One thing they say is, 'It's not necessary for any man to be a crow'. My interpretation of that is that you don't have to act like something you're not, or be less than you are, or disbelieve yourself."

Lee sits down again and flicks through a few more pages. On one is a poem which begins: "A painter is sat in an old vintage village; Quietly looking for inspiration". But he's looking for something else. Eventually he finds it. It's another poem, but this time it's not in Lee's distinctive scrawl. It's untitled, but 'Brussels' is written at the top of the page. It begins:

Have you ever felt the strength of silence
Banging inside your head?
Did it make you angry or did it create
More doubts for you instead?
It's for you to unravel everything
Kept inside of time
To be seen and to disconnect
All you've been taught to respect
And understand your own individual thoughts.

It finishes: "It's the biggest battle of them all. It's you against you." Underneath, in the same handwriting, is written:

Hi,
Thanks for a great and different night. By being inspired you'll be able to give that same magic to another and that is a great gift! I wish you all the best, success within your career. But mostly peace and strength inside your heart.
See you soon, somewhere.

"Liz went mad over that," Lee says – it turns out the poem and the message had both been written by a girl while Lee had been on the road during his relationship with Atomic Kitten's Liz McClarnon. "She thought there was something going on, but nothing like that happened at all. I just met her when I was out of this country and we had this really long chat. Like, for hours. And it was really unlike chatting with the kind of people you usually meet when you're on the road. It was difficult explaining that kind of thing to Liz." He pauses to reflect on his time with the girl. After a while, he asks, "Did she put her number in there, too?"

But she didn't; all that's left of the mystery girl is the message and a memory of an evening spent with someone whose connection was more deep and fulfilling than a one night stand or stolen snog in a club. And Lee is forced to concede that sometimes these people, inspirational people who will never know how they've affected your life, just flit into your life and then, just as suddenly, they disappear, sometimes never to be seen again.

To the outsider it might seem strange that this book

is the property of the same Lee Ryan who whiles away his spare time attempting to knock over Portaloos with his mates inside.

"I suppose it does go against the image everyone has of me," Lee says. "But sometimes I'd rather people thought I was an idiot than knew exactly what I was about. There're some people I don't want inside my head."

Perhaps the Lee who scribbles in this book is the Lee Ryan the mainstream media don't want you to see: after all, poetry doesn't sell newspapers. But Lee explains that it's his creativity which keeps him sane. "That's why I stayed in the studio on my birthday," he says. "I couldn't really handle going out and I didn't want to go out. I just wanted to have a bit of fun and the only way I could think of having fun was by sitting in the studio. Which is what I did. I was just sat there all night, singing, writing. It was great."

Picking his way through the backstage buffet, Johnny B – a veteran of these events – explains how difficult the backstage areas can sometimes be. "Party In The Park is well organised," he begins, "and it has to be, just because of its size and the number of bands who are onstage during the day. But this year I think the backstage area is lacking a certain something…"

It's easy to see what he means. It seems that every summer, as more and more pop acts barge their way on to the music scene and more and more events like Party In The Park spring up around the country, things like this are becoming a lot more chaotic. Up-and-coming acts – and there are many here today, some not even appearing onstage – are desperate to get their music to as many fans as possible, zooming up and down the country in their Previas from mimed PA to mimed PA.

"This year it seems that people are just turning up, doing their thing and then clearing off again immediately," Johnny says, nodding. "Blue are here all day, but because there's no real transport for the bands to come and go from the site, they're finding themselves wedged in the VIP area."

Ah yes, the VIP area. 'VIP' has become a bit of a loose term, which is good on one hand because it means that friends, family and distant relatives of the PITP guestlist can all mingle backstage. But it also means that it can be difficult for a band to find any space to relax. Everyone, it seems, has a Blue fan in their life: a niece, a nephew, a next-door-neighbour's long-lost grandson. Even so, the boys are thrilled to be here. Simon remembers the band's first ever Party In The Park fondly.

"Oh, man," he gasps as he casts his mind back. "Our *first* Party In The Park. I think we were pretty lucky to even get on the bill for that one, we were still so new. Our performance went so quick that I don't even remember going on! It was just so surreal, seeing all these massive acts all getting on with each other in the same place." Si adds that the people who put the event together have been really good to Blue in the years since that first performance – every year their time on stage has extended a little bit more. And today, with a five song set booked in, Blue are providing the show's second-to-last performance. (The last one will be the cast of the West End musical *Grease* banging through their biggest numbers – the perfect climax to a lazy Sunday in Hyde Park.)

While Duncan's off with the film crew doing another live piece to the Channel 5 audience, Simon takes a stroll around the side of the stage and up into the wings. The view from the stage is awesome. "Look at that!" he yells, pointing to somewhere in the distance, "it's just a sea of people! It just goes on forever. You feel like going 'Hey, you dudes at the back there, can you see me, let alone hear me? It's madness."

It's difficult from up here to make out the individual faces in the crowd, but we know that there's one very famous face here somewhere, and it belongs to Prince Charles. Unlike a lot of the summer's pop roadshows, Party In The Park isn't just a promotional tool for a radio station or a couple of grand in a promoter's back pocket, but the opportunity to raise hundreds and hundreds of thousands of pounds for The Prince's Trust, which focuses its attentions on 14- to 30-year-olds, building their confidence, helping them find their directions in life and in many cases giving them the necessary backing to start off in business. So far almost half a million young people have benefited from The Prince's Trust, getting them off the streets, off the drugs, out of whatever's holding them back in life.

"I've seen things like drugs and stuff that go on around me," Simon says. "Not necessarily my friends, but definitely friends of friends... I was lucky in a way, 'cos we was all anti-drugs because we were sportsmen. I was a footballer when I was growing up so drugs was like a thing where it was like, 'Ugh, get that away from me. I don't want to be around you when you're doing that.' I was a health freak for a long time, though that's sort of slid a bit now! But I know that for a load of kids, growing up is a really tough time. *Real* tough. It means such a lot to be a part of something like this, to be maybe making a direct difference to someone's life."

Simon has some strong views on what it means to be young and, as a father himself, he has the nation's youth on his mind an awful lot. He launches into a long monologue. It infuriates him, and confuses him, that kids are growing up without learning how to write; how every individual has their individuality knocked out of them at school. He finds it baffling that every teenager speaks like a character from *Dawson's Creek*. And he's not too fond of technology, either.

"Right," he begins. You get the impression this will be a long point. "Yeah, times change, but kids have got to be kids, man. They've got to know about going out to parks and building tree houses and building tents and building ramps for their bikes." He waves his hand at an imaginary teenager. "Go to a park on the swings and hang out, for God's sake! Don't be behind a computer when the sun's out and you could be out working your lungs! Getting fit! That's what I'll be doing with my kids. My kids won't even know what a computer is until it's time. If you want to go out, go down the Trocadero. Meet people. Go and make some friends. Don't the parents realise that, as this generation grows up, they'll become boxed in and have no identity? Nobody will be able to relate to anyone. Even now, if you listen to kids, they're just talking about computers and what's going on on the Internet! I had a good upbringing – a good, social upbringing. I used to go to the dump and get old doors and wheels, and make things out of them. Or when there was, like, 14 of us, we used to go to another area and find people playing football and challenge them. 'Us lot against your lot,' we'd say. 'All right,' they'd say. That was a part of growing up. That was a part of being streetwise and knowing what's going on in the streets as well and what's cool. I miss those days, boy. What we used to get up to…" The rant is over. Simon's locked in a stroll down memory lane. "Those days," he finishes. "They were madness." He wanders off in search of Beyoncé Knowles, with marriage in mind.

In Channel 5's TV studio, Dunc's doing some links

for the viewers at home. It's live TV, so things happen which weren't in the script (at one point the sound on a video tape is interrupted by Denise Van Outen screaming "WHAT'S GOING ON?!" into a live micro-phone), and there are some funny moments when members of the public are phoning in with their opinions. In one instance, Duncan had trouble keeping a straight face:

Denise: "So, who are you looking forward to seeing onstage today?"

Caller: "Big Brovaz and Beyoncé."

Denise: "And *(gesturing towards Duncan)* what about Blue?"

Caller: "Er... *(Long pause.)* Yeah, all right. And Blue."

As the sun's beginning to drop from the sky, Duncan, *Big Brother* winner (and Capital FM DJ, TV presenter and Dunc's friend) Kate Lawler and Denise get on the stage to greet the 100,000 strong Party In The Park audience. Kate decides that the crowd should all cheer for Duncan to take off his shirt – which he does, to reveal another T-shirt. It has 'I [heart] Kate' written on it, which sends the audience utterly bonkers and prompts Denise to wonder out loud whether Dunc will take *that* shirt off, too. Caught up in the moment, that's precisely what he does. "Ooh," Denise gasps, "*he's* not shy, is he?" She's right – and with a sniff of the armpit, Dunc lobs his T-shirt into the crowd, where it's pounced upon by a gaggle of fans. The rest of the crowd are staring up at Duncan's naked torso on the stage's huge TV screens.

Before long it's stagetime, and thirty seconds before they're due on the band huddle in the wings, slap a mountain of hands down in the centre of their circle then throw them skywards with a charming cry of "ONE! TWO! THREE! BOLLOCKS!", a pre-show ritual we'll be hearing a lot of over the next couple of months. And then they're on!

During the performance, Simon bursts into a rap. It's difficult to make out above the thudding basslines and the screaming fans, but it goes like this:

Radiate the darkness for rising suns
And dedicate this to the fans who have been
   there since day one
Look how far we've come and it's down to you
Giving us support through album one, album two

We work so hard for the glory and the fame
Now out of the blue, you're trying to take our
   name?
12 million albums, there's only one Blue
It's not about the name, it's the things we do

Back to reality, rock, spitting mad flows
Back to Hyde Park, spitting hot flows
And back to back Brit Awards, that's how it goes.
And what's the verdict?
Case closed.

Eventually the band leave the stage to thunderous applause and they're buzzing so much that they want to go right back out there again, but there's plenty more to be done, and backstage, although the show's almost over, the atmosphere is still electric. The band are whisked to a backstage area where a live broadcast on Channel 5 climaxes as Lee pulls down his trousers and moons at millions of teenage TV viewers.

He writes poetry too, though, y'know.

*   *   *

A week after Party In The Park we're at Manchester Airport, on a day where the weather can't make up its mind what to do. When we pull up outside and head inside in search of Duncan it's sunny; five minutes later when there's no sign of Duncan but there's a swarm of traffic wardens buzzing around the car, it's dumping it down with rain. When we eventually find Duncan he's wandering around the airport's small arrivals lounge and, while the occasional eagle-eyed fan is asking for an autograph, a grey hoodie, pulled-down cap and baggy combats ensure that his anonymity is almost total. He bounds up and greets us with a cheery hello, revitalised by a few days out of the Blue whirlwind.

"I'm knackered, but it was a great couple of days," he smiles. "And sometimes two days away is all it takes." He fiddles with his mobile. "Know where I can get a top-up card?"

Obviously, the idea of any pop celebrity – let alone one in the UK's biggest boyband – having to muddle along with a pay-as-you-go mobile is faintly ridiculous, but Dunc's off on a top-up card hunt and eventually finds a kiosk. Even then he has to rummage around in his pockets for the right money – eventually finding ten quid of the correct currency and whacking the card in his phone. Almost immediately the mobile springs to life with the dozens of texts, voicemails and missed calls accumulated during his short time on the plane.

We leave the terminal: the car hasn't been towed away yet, which is a relief, but it's still raining. Dunc surveys the cloudy sky. "Welcome back to England," he smiles, as he jumps in the back of the Chrysler and begins to rummage in his bag. From among the hand luggage debris – deodorant, notebooks and diaries –

he rescues a copy of today's *Sun* newspaper and a packet of salt and vinegar square crisps, both of which he begins to devour. "So, what's been happening while I've been away?" he wonders out loud as he thumbs through the newspaper. The answer, he soon discovers, is not much at all: but the new round of *Fame Academy* contestants, one of whom will probably be doing battle with Blue in this Christmas's Top 10, has been revealed. Duncan seems more interested in his packet of crisps.

As we pull out of the airport leaving the Malaga sunshine (and a flurry of traffic wardens) far behind, Duncan turns his attentions to that mobile phone, juggling calls and flicking between conversations with a roll-call of disjointed voices on the other end. "Hi babe, I'm back"... "That suit fitting's changed from 4pm? Til when?"... "Nah, we should have really messy hair for the shoot"... "Make sure the clothes are really edgy looking"... "Are you still there? Hello?"

Today's plan is fairly simple: we've picked up

Duncan *en route* to Liverpool, where he'll meet up with the rest of the band and perform at the second of Blue's Liverpool Summer Pops shows. The roads are clear and the journey will only take 45 minutes, but Duncan needs sleep, and every second of this not-quite-an-hour of shut-eye will count. He clears his bag and clutter off the back seat of the Chrysler and takes a lie down. Inevitably, within seconds, the phone is ringing. It's Tara Palmer-Tomkinson, and even here in the front of the car you can hear her excited babbling on the other end of the line. She's just heard that an influential magazine have got wind of her and Duncan's new business venture – and they want to interview the pair. Duncan flips his phone shut. "That's *such* wicked news," he gushes and goes on to explain everything about the new company he and Tara have set up.

"Basically," he says, "I've gone into partnership with Tara, in a TV production company called Meltdown. It's something I've always wanted to do – something outside music – because TV, acting and drama are in many ways where my roots are. Tara was looking for the same thing, so it made perfect sense, really."

"We've already got our feet in the door," Duncan says, "and we're working on some really great shows already." He explains that one of the shows is a Saturday night, prime time format. "There's some pretty bad TV shows around," Dunc says. "But I know what I like and Tara knows what she likes, and we've both got the ideas." He adds that they're going for 'water-cooler moments', those pieces of television which become hot topics of office conversation on a Monday morning. "It's just the killer idea," Dunc says. "It's not about the money. Ideas cost nothing, but they're the currency in good TV."

Time for more sleep. It's difficult there on the back seat, but if you can't actually get to sleep you might as well assume the position.

Our driver is Martin, who's helping Johnny B with today's driving duties. He's been on the road since 6.30am, driving up from his home in Kent, but his senses are still razor-sharp and with Duncan asleep he gets on to another portion of the group's entourage. They're already in Liverpool and Ant, in particular, is making the most of an Elvis Presley exhibition round the corner from the venue. But before we can meet up with Ant and the lads, we need to drop off Duncan. To make sure that his performance in tonight's show is as good as possible, he decides that he'll miss out the soundcheck and sleep through for as long as possible – also giving him a chance to rest his voice, which is feeling a bit strained after his flight from Malaga. Eventually we pull up at the Liverpool Marriott, and Dunc leaps out of the car, grabs his bag and checks into the hotel. It's the last we'll see of him for a few hours.

Twenty minutes later we arrive at Liverpool's Albert Dock, at 1.25 million square feet, the largest Grade 1 listed building in Britain. The Dock was built in 1846 and opened by Prince Albert, and soon buzzed with massive trade ships taking wares in and out of the UK.

It closed as a working dock in 1972, and these days it's full of gift centres and tourist attractions. Richard and Judy used to host their morning chat-shows from studios built into the docks themselves and their legacy – a huge floating map of Great Britain, across which a hapless weatherman would often bound and occasionally fall into the water – still remains. We walk past the Beatles exhibition in search of Elvis, an artist who has rather less to do with Liverpool than Ringo, George, Paul and John but whose influence is maybe felt more in today's pop charts. We discover Antony milling around in the Elvis exhibition bookshop, stocking up with a carrier bag full of memorabilia including a large portrait of Elvis for his fiancée. On the way out he's accosted by a woman and her two teenage daughters: they want autographs.

Having cleaned out the merchandise stall, we make our way past the Richard and Judy map ("I never once saw that fool fall in!" Ant guffaws, a little dejectedly) and down to the venue. This is the first year of the Liverpool

Summer Pops – a huge event for the local community and one which has already seen appearances from artists as diverse as the Sugababes and Atomic Kitten and, on the other hand, old favourites like ZZ Top (notable mainly for their huge beards, in spite of the fact that the only member whose surname is Beard doesn't actually have one), Status Quo (popularised denim and ponytails on men in the seventies), and Lesley Garratt (the nearest the opera community has to a Madonna). Of all these acts, with tens of millions of records sold between them, Blue are the only band to be playing twice.

In spite of this, there's a bit of confusion once we're in, as a security fella strolls up to Antony.

"'Ere, don't you need a VIP wristband? Are you here with that Blue lot?"

Antony laughs. "Yeah mate, I'm *in* Blue."

The guard looks a little embarrassed. "Ooooh!" he laughs. "I'm a Villa supporter!"

A confused look flashes across Ant's face. What has any of this got to do with football? Either way, he gets his wristband and, with Antony saved from being hurled from the site, the show is saved.

We decide to take a look around the venue, which is actually a massive green and yellow circus tent. Inside it looks a bit like a mini-me version of Wembley or any of the massive venues around the country but the immediate backstage area, in spite of being under canvas, is a little more plush. It's carpeted, for a start, and there's a massive grand piano there, though it's been turned on its side and had a huge blanket draped over it, as if that would somehow disguise the piano's abuse. The gravelly artist area is right behind the tent itself, and seems to have been modelled on the Seven Wonders Of The World, or at least some wonders which should have made the Top Seven. Certainly there are some strange replicas of the Easter Island stone heads, and there's a water feature and a couple of bushes which, at a push, could be the Hanging Gardens of Babylon, except for the fact that they're not hanging and not really in Babylon. They're in Liverpool: 'THE

WORLD IN ONE CITY' according to a sign strapped proudly to a fence, though the weather is, simply, British. There are some park benches scattered around too, though nobody seems to sit on these, and the air is rich with the scent of fish: nothing to do with being by the docks, everything to do with this afternoon's late lunch menu. Backstage is buzzing with Blue's support acts for the day: local girl Jennifer Ellison fresh from the Top 10 success of her debut single, and more local talent in the shape of Eurovision failures Jemini, who appear to be spending most of their time screaming and whooping their way around the place.

In Blue's own dressing room, Ant's getting busy with a black marker pen, following in the footsteps of all the acts who've already appeared at the Summer Pops festival so far this summer, and signing his name on posters, books and two massive leather sofas. Ant surveys the names scrawled around the room: The Beach Boys, James Brown, Paul Weller, er, Fast Food Rockers. He looks up at a huge poster on the wall featuring every act of the summer. He's counting in his head. Eventually he turns to Johnny B. "So why are we the only ones doing two shows?"

Johnny laughs. "Ticket sales, mate," he says. "You're popular."

Martin, our driver, suddenly remembers that he has a surprise for Ant, and dashes off to his car. He comes back wielding the *Lock, Stock And Two Smoking Barrels* soundtrack CD and, after wrestling with the eject button on a dressing room CD player, finally finds the track he's after: 'Zorba The Greek'. In the seventies the song's composer, Mikis Theodorakis, was thrown in prison for opposing military rule and the song was banned, so he'd no doubt be over the moon to know how happy the song makes Ant feel. He immediately springs to life, jumping around the Portakabin with what is probably best described as a 'unique' Greek dance interpretation of the song. For the next 15 minutes he sits contentedly on the sofa with the remote control, flicking between tracks and his favourite snatches of *Lock, Stock* dialogue, mouthing along to his favourites. "They're like kids, sometimes," muses Johnny from the corner of the room. When he's finished, Ant decides he wants to listen to a Paul Weller CD but, when it becomes obvious that his flicking between *Lock, Stock* tracks has left the stereo well and truly knackered, he decides to take matters into his own hands. "Let's go and cause a fuss in the production office!" he roars. "Their CD player's eaten *Lock, Stock*!" He peers out of the door at the downpour outside. "On second thoughts, let's just stay in here." Lee's driving up in his new Porsche, and Simon's on his way from London having finished filming a TV appearance. "No wonder I'm the one they always call Rolex," Ant sighs – it is, he says, because he's always on time.

While Ant picks at the selection of nuts and nibbles on offer, someone manages to prise the CD player open and put in what they think is the long-awaited Paul Weller CD. Within seconds it becomes obvious that it's something altogether more horrifying – a compilation of pop hits whose cheese factor is off the scale. Track One is 'Making Your Mind Up' by Bucks Fizz, the band who represented Britain in Eurovision while Jemini were still in nappies. Ant whacks the volume up and, for a brief moment, it seems utterly hilarious. The joke starts to wear off, yet the CD remains on and the sounds of Steps, Abba and assorted disco greats create a rather strange air in the Blue dressing room.

At 5.30pm, Lee's arrival on site is heralded by the Blue dancers chanting 'Leeeeeeeee! Leeeeeeeee!', like the green *Toy Story* aliens, as he bounds through the gates. He sees Ant – launches himself into the air, tries to wrestle him to the floor, fails, lets out a massive laugh. Now the fans lined up on the other side of the security fence have caught wind of the fact that Lee's on site: "LEEEEEEE! LEEEEEEE!" Lee runs into the Portakabin and throws himself on a sofa. After a couple of seconds he sits bolt upright. "Can I have a cup of tea?"

Simon also arrives, straight from London. He's been

recording a show for Flaunt TV, called *Select A Beau*, in which a fan gets to date either Simon, David Sneddon, Jamie from Triple 8 or Abs. Si explains that he, Abs and Jamie tried to engineer it so that the fan, who was a Sneddo obsessive, got to go on the date with David, and muses on his role as a lust object. "I try not to believe my own hype too much," he says as he unpacks his bag. "That kind of thing can be flattering, and I remember having crushes when I was a kid, so I know where they're coming from." Perhaps ill-advisedly, Si reveals that his childhood crush was hilarious Hollywood superbitch Joan Collins.

As the crowds start filing into the tent, things are hotting up backstage. There's a knock on the dressing room door – will the boys come out to sign some autographs? Lee pokes his head out to find to fans – both in wheelchairs, both called Christina, both decked out in Blue T-shirts and both draped in flags and banners, waiting patiently outside. He skips down the steps and plants a big, wet kiss on each set of cheeks.

One of the Christinas' mums pulls Lee aside. "I'll tell you what Lee, I'm sick of the sound of you," she begins. Suddenly things sound like they might be turning a bit awkward. "Morning, noon and night, all I hear is Blue." She lets out a laugh. Lee lets out a laugh. The two Christinas guffaw wildly. Lee poses for a pic with the fans and the Christina on the left tugs his shirt. "Lee, can I ask you something?"

"Course you can, love."

"Is Duncan here?"

Duncan, of course, is still asleep at the hotel. Moments later, Simon appears from the dancers' dressing room with a huge grin on his face. "I just been layin' me bombs," he smiles. Blank faces all round. Turns out that's where he goes when he needs a fart! By 8pm, the atmosphere in the tent is off the scale. Some acts have already been onstage and others – well, one in particular – are yet to come. Dunc finally arrives from the hotel looking refreshed and ready to put in an amazing performance. By 20 past, the whole band are in the dressing room with their tops – and in Ant's and Si's cases, their trousers – off, getting ready for the show with vocal coach Stevie Lange. She's trying to create a feeling of calm in the dressing room, but every time the door opens the crowd's screaming bursts in like a force ten gale and, anyway, with Lee around any feeling of calm is pretty brief. Especially because he's just realised that he's left his car lights on. While someone's despatched with his keys to sort it out, Lee flings himself to the floor and knocks out ten press-ups – partly to get the adrenalin pumping, partly because it's *already* pumping. Now all of the lads are doing their exercises – but chaos reigns. Phones ring (usually answered with "I'm just about to go on!" – Click), fans blunder in demanding autographs and posed photos. Lee's exercise regime is on to its next step now: he's horizontal with his feet on one chair and his arms holding him up on another, doing backwards push-ups. When he's finished he locks arms with Simon – they push each others' arms up, then down, then up again, then Lee gets back down on the floor for more press-ups.

Dunc's the last of the lads to get changed, so he's struggling with jeans and a T-shirt while doing his vocal warm-ups at the same time. Stevie's still at her keyboard, leading the boys in chants and choruses to warm up their muscles. *"Yeeeeahhhh-hhhhhhhh!"* she wails, a distant echo of Lulu's 'Shout'. The boys follow suit. *"I feeeeeeeeel goood!"* Each of the different phrases warms up the boys in a different way. Next, Stevie reaches for her Thermos flask and pours each of the boys a mug of her special recipe lemon and ginger drink. As she reaches to pass Simon his, Duncan announces terrible news. "My throat is really bad," he suddenly announces. The room falls silent. Even with just 15 minutes until the lads are due on stage, Stevie remains unflapped.

"OK, Duncan," she begins, "you're going to be fine. What I want you to do is just *slide* your voice between the notes. Don't be aggressive with them, just slide…"

Dunc has a go, and it sounds fine. But he's not happy. "Sorry, love, it's not going to work. My voice is wrecked."

Undaunted, Stevie concentrates on Duncan for another five minutes, taking him through more warm-ups until he's ready to perform.

Watching from the corner, Johnny B explains how important it is that the boys sing live – and how that means it's such a disaster when their voices go. "We once turned up for a gig with only three quarters of the band, because one of their throats was shot right through," he says. "It was an awful predicament: we didn't want to let the fans down, and we knew that a lot of other bands would often try to pull a fast one and just not turn up at all. The thing with Blue is that they hate miming. But we talked to the people at the gig, explained to the fans, and the three other lads did the show by themselves."

Simon's at one end of the room totally silent, sealed off in the strict world of Tai Chi exercises. The movements are slight, but by the end his body's coiled like a spring, and he's sweating.

Dunc's also talking about Ant's engagement party that weekend – it was great, he says, because "it gave me the chance to be around people, where I didn't have to be anybody but myself". The way he says it is almost sad, as if he knows the days of social anonymity are long gone.

"It's one of the best parties I've ever been to," Simon agrees. "We were surrounded by friends and there was no press. Actually, every time Ant has a party, it's always great. He knows how to put on a party, that kid."

"Cheers mate," Ant laughs. "It was a really long, hectic day, but I had an amazing time. All my friends were there, all the ones that I'd grown up with. I was crying because I was so happy."

Since the band will be 'doing a runner' tonight – which is to say that when they leave the stage they'll literally sprint from the venue, through the backstage area and into a waiting car with the motor running –

they're having to pack their stuff before they go on stage. The fridge is raided for whatever remaining beers there are for the journeys home and the last few packets of crisps are stored in bags. By the time the band leave the Portakabin, it looks like it's been burgled.

From outside, Antony pokes his head into the dressing room. "Awright lads? Why are we hanging around in here? Is the show cancelled or something? Hahaha!" Ant's lifted the mood and, with just a couple of minutes left until the band are live on stage, they're walked through a flap in the back of the tent and into the carpeted interior. The dancers are already there, decked out in their basketball-themed costumes and chucking the balls around at each other as the lads have their 'ears' – those one-sided headphone things which allow you to hear what you're singing above the echo of what you sang a second ago, and which therefore prevent the entire live show from going tits up – installed.

The curtain drops (and gets caught, as they often do, requiring someone to yank it down), and the lads open with 'Riders' – one of Si's favourite songs from the *One Love* album and a delicious taste of where the lads are heading with their new album. Except nobody in the audience knows that yet and, despite the fact that there's no new material in tonight's set, there's a buoyancy and an energy to the performance which gives each song new life.

As the dancers leave the stage it's time for Lee to make a special announcement to the people of Liverpool. "We want to thank each and every one of you," he says to some quiet screams. "'Cos if it wasn't for you" *(louder screams)*, "we wouldn't be… Stood here today!" *(Place goes utterly bonkers.)* He could, of course, say the same thing every night to every venue in the country, and to a certain degree he does, but this is never an excuse for getting a cheap scream from the audience. When pop bands launch, they are always accessible – in fact, with school tours, impromptu club appearances and signings at tiny little record stores, the bands actually go to the fans, or at least to the potential fans. Almost always, the instant that band becomes even slightly successful those fans are forgotten, left behind as the band become complacent, 'too important' to talk to the actual people who buy the records. Sure, they'll talk about 'the fans' in interviews, and they'll stop to sign autographs when they know there's a photographer around to capture the moment and pass it on to seven million newspaper readers, but when it comes down to it fans are often forgotten and the things some bands say about their fans behind closed doors is astonishing. Something which does make Blue quite different from some of their peers is that when they do stop a gig and say thanks to their fans, they mean it.

As one song ends Lee leans into the audience, which soon becomes a forest of grasping hands, grasps a fan's drink and takes a cheeky swig before handing it back. "Thanks, love," he says to the fan, and to the entire audience.

Dunc introduces 'Too Close' and tells the audience

that it's for "all the ladies in the room", chiefly because this is their opportunity to sing – and sing they do, on one of those songs which actually sounds better with a bit of a live twist than it does on record. Then there's 'All Rise', and 'Sorry Seems To Be The Hardest Word', which sounds electric even without the presence of Sir Elton. When it comes to 'One Love', Simon has a message: "I'm not gonna preach, but that's a song with a message. No matter what colour or where you're from, we all breathe the same air so let's get along."

The banners in tonight's audience – 'DUNC U MAKE ME WANNA', and so on – are thankfully quite tame by the standards of some we've seen, but one in the front row does catch Lee's eye: "LEE – MARRY ME". He pauses between two songs and points it out to the rest of the audience. "Well," he ponders. "*Should I get married?*" You could hear a pin drop. "Awright then," Lee adds with a shrug of the shoulders. He gets the message, loud and clear: 'Don't get married, Lee. Well, not unless it's to me.' "Don't worry, girls," he announces, "Liverpool girls are the best" – adding, in reference to his relationship with Liz Kitten, "and you know I'm prone to a Liverpool girl." At which point he hurls his towel into the crowd, causing a minor stampede as the 300 fans in the vicinity scramble to get a piece of it. Heaven only knows what drama would have unfolded had Lee thrown his mobile number into the crowd, but before there's time to ponder, Lee's already up the scaffolding, causing a minor security alert.

They leave the stage to a riot of applause and, as per usual, everyone sprints out, jumps straight into their cars and speeds off. Well, everyone except Lee. Fifteen minutes after Antony, Simon and Duncan have left the site, he's still in the dressing room, milling around. In fact, when we walk in, he's butt naked trying to find his boxer shorts – chatting away with Stevie Lange. "Lee!" booms Johnny B from outside. "Get your arse out of there and get home!"

Except he doesn't do that, either: half an hour later while the dancers and musicians are waiting for their own tourbus, Lee's still screaming around. As the driver boots two teenage girls from the bus (they wanted him to "take us to Amsterdam and show us a good time"; he politely declined), Lee claws open the side door and jumps on, running up and down the corridor and terrorising the dancers. At the front of the bus, he finds a three-year-old daughter of one of the dancers, hoists her on to his shoulders, and goes for a stroll around the carpark, walking right up to the thin wire fence separating him from hundreds of screaming fans. "LEEEEEEEE!!! LEEEEE!" goes the roar; he has time to sign two autographs before security tell him to "get back on the bloody bus" before the fence gives way. Once back on the bus he puts the child down, bids everyone a chirpy goodbye and disappears through the side door. The next anybody sees of Lee that night is a blue Porsche tearing out of the carpark and into the cold Liverpool night, destination London.

On the way back, Lee's strangely silent, though he does talk a little about politics. "I wouldn't want to be a politician," he begins. "I get the hump too much! Then again, if I was given the chance I'd have a good go at it. My policies? They'd be against everything else. Except the stuff that was good."

While this might sound a little vague, Lee's views on education make a little more sense. "When you're at school you're taught what to learn, not *how* to learn. I never did well at school. Art is one of the big controversial things at school. They teach you how to draw, not be an artist. When I was at school I was told I had to draw an egg. I was, like, 'I don't want to draw an egg.' They went, 'But it'll teach you how to shade.' I said, 'But I already know how to shade, and I do it like *this*.' 'But that's the wrong way to shade. The real artists don't shade like that.' It's stupid."

*　　*　　*

Saturday, 26 July has two parts. In the first instalment the boys will be performing at the gay and lesbian extravaganza Pride In The Park (which has been called Mardi Gras for the past few years and is still unofficially know as such), and in the second they'll be appearing at G-A-Y at the London Astoria.

As we pull up towards the Pride In The Park entrance, there's a sea of umbrellas. It's pouring down with rain. When you're as busy as a band like Blue, you have to make the most of every second you get to yourself, and in the four minutes between entering Hyde Park's first gate and driving through the VIP artist entrance, Duncan has somehow persuaded the driver to pick up his car next week and take it to be serviced.

We jump out of the car and walk into the backstage area, which is strewn with Portakabins, portable toilets and puddles of muddy water from the day's heavy rain. More of today's performers are milling around, either getting ready to perform or having just come off stage, which is in the same place as Party In The Park earlier this month, except a bit smaller. Danish dance popsters Junior Senior are in the dressing room to one side of

Blue's, and on the other side are Mis-teeq. Over the walkway are Appleton, Javine and the cast of a lesbian musical called *Always The Bride*.

As soon as we get into the dressing room, a runner pokes his head around the door and gives Blue their thirty minute warning, setting the band machine whirring into action. Maarit sets at Ant's hair with a pair of hair straightners while the band's dancers run around trying to locate their costumes.

Johnny B appears. He's been outside, and up on to the stage, checking out the conditions, and he has a word of warning for everyone who'll be on stage today. "Right, everyone, listen up. It's wet out there. The wind isn't blowing the rain on to the stage, but the stage is still soaking. I don't want anyone out there doing anything stupid – if you can't do your routines without slipping over, just don't do your routines." Everyone takes heed of Johnny's advice; after all, the last thing anyone wants to see is Blue in an Avid Merrion-style neck brace.

As ever, the event organisers are making the most

of having Blue on the premises. As well as the performance on stage this afternoon, the lads have been
booked for a string of radio and TV interviews between
now and the performance. Right now, a journalist from
Radio One is in the Blue Portakabin trying to interview
Dunc. He's doing something he'll spend a lot of time
doing over the next few months: not so much talking
about the band's plan, as clearing up the rumours and
speculation which follow the band wherever they go. As
he chats amiably with Radio One and records station
idents for their various shows ("Hello, my name is
Duncan, I'm in a band called Blue and you're listening
to *The Sunday Surgery*…"), at the same time he's trying
to cope with Maarit and her hair straighteners, above
the noise of Ant throwing strawberries at the dancers
and the rest of the entourage attempting to open
bottles of beer without a bottle-opener. (After various
unsuccessful methods, Dunc eventually has his bottle
opened by a fan – using his teeth!) With 20 minutes until
stagetime, it comes as a surprise to precisely nobody

that Lee has gone AWOL. Ten minutes before stagetime he's eventually found chatting with Mis-teeq in the next door Portakabin. With not long to go, the finishing touches are put to the band's stage costumes – today they've gone for a military look with khaki vests and the last addition is a thin layer of baby oil for some on-stage glistening. Mind you, there's little need for any extra moisture today, seeing as the rain is still showering down on Hyde Park.

The Mardi Gras runner pushes his head round the door again. "THREE MINUTES!"

Typically Duncan decides that now is the time for a pee, but we make our way round through the soggy VIP area to the side of the stage just in time. The event is being compared by ex-*SM:TV* host Brian Dowling and Pride In The Park promoter Jeremy Joseph, who's been responsible for getting Blue on the bill today. As the pair rattle through their introduction ("There's a cheeky one called Duncan, there's one with a great body called Simon," and so on), someone standing next to Lee at the side of the stage decides, for reasons best known to himself, that now is the time for a card trick, and produces a pack of cards from his pocket. "Pick a card!" he bellows, with a flourish.

"Sorry mate, I'm just about to go on!" Lee yells back.

"Go on, it won't take long!" Magicians can be very insistent, you see. So Lee picks a card from the pack. Takes a look at it. Puts it back in the pack. The magician shuffles the pack, and selects one of the cards just as Brian Dowling yells "...please welcome onstage, BLUE!"

"Is this your card, Lee?"

Lee's already running for the stage, but sees the card. "NOOOOO!" he calls back as he disappears up the steps – and he's right. It's not his card. What a rubbish trick. There's just time for the lads' chant of "ONE! TWO! THREE! BOLLOCKS!" before they're out on the stage before thousands of screaming fans.

As Blue begin their time on stage, Jeremy Joseph comes off. Jeremy also runs London's massive G-A-Y club night, and has booked Blue to play there on many,

many occasions. Tonight they'll be on at the ungodly hour of two in the morning. Jeremy says that he's pleased as punch that the lads are referring to today as 'Blue's Gay Day', and scurries off to find the next band due on stage. Out at the front of the stage, the Pride In The Park revellers are making the most of a fairly unpleasant day. It hasn't been raining much so far this week so the grass isn't too waterlogged, but it's still grim underfoot and people are either avoiding the main walkways, where the ground's really churned up, or diving into the mud headfirst. A few tents have been pitched near to the stage and look like they're in a bit of danger of floating off, but a large crowd are still gathered at the stage, refusing to let the weather prevent them from having a good time.

Watching from the side of the stage, Johnny B recalls one gig the boys played a couple of years ago where the rain was *really* bad. "They were supporting Santana at Crystal Palace," he recalls. "The rain was just torrential and the wind was blowing on to the stage so all the equipment was getting wet. We thought everyone was going to get fried! And then inevitably, as soon as the boys came off stage, the rain stopped, the sun came out and it was fantastic. We left and went home, wringing wet."

"I know it's raining," Lee says to the crowd. "But we're here to have a good time... So *scream*!" The crowd, who are also acutely aware that it's raining, let out a huge scream, as Blue launch into 'All Rise'. Quite surreally, while the lads' dancers today are all blokes, there is one woman on stage. She's right at the front, to one side of the stage, and looks for a while as if she might be doing her own dance routine to 'All Rise'. As it turns out, she's actually interpreting the song's lyrics in sign language for the benefit of the audience's deaf members, and has been there all day doing the same for all the other acts on the main stage. How well she coped with interpreting Alesha from Mis-teeq's speedy raps is not known, though she gets 'All Rise' down to a tee.

The lads storm through 'Fly By', and then 'One Love', which Simon introduces with the usual spiel about the song having a meaning, but at today's event it does have a real sense of significance. As Simon points out, "Today really is all about one love." After 'You Make Me Wanna' the boys run off stage, and back to the Portakabin. They're happy with their perform-ance and feel that they made the most of the slippery conditions. There's one problem, though: behind the curtain on stage, someone was banging a drum during Blue's performance. They decide to point the finger at Junior Senior.

There are a couple more interviews to be done, but as soon as they're out of the way Johnny B is keen that the lads get off the site as soon as possible. "Come on, boys, clear off!" he bellows. Johnny probably hopes the lads will all go back to have some sleep in advance of tonight's (i.e. tomorrow morning's) G-A-Y appearance, though of course it's Saturday night and nobody's thinking about being sensible. Each of the boys is on his mobile making arrangements with friends to meet in town, and we arrange to meet round the back of G-A-Y at 1am. In the ten years since it was invented, G-A-Y has become an institution. Before 1993, London's gay clubbing scene was a bit of a snobby affair, but when Jeremy Joseph opened the doors to his new club there was suddenly a place where people could go without having to be worried about how cool they were. The G-A-Y empire is continually expanding, and Saturday nights are held at the Astoria, a London venue with loads of history all of its own. It's hosted gigs by everyone from old favourites like U2 and the Rolling Stones, to pop talents like Kylie Minogue and Christina Aguilera, and it has the distinct whiff of indie about it.

Because today is Gay Day not just for Blue but for the entire country too, G-A-Y have put on a special show tonight and, rather than the usual one or two acts, there'll be five. When Blue get to their dressing room, they discover that they'll be sharing with another band. It's not any of the other acts on tonight's bill, which includes US teen popstrel Kaci, chart-toppers Junior Senior and dance diva and DJ, Ultra Nate. It turns out the band who'll be sharing Blue's red dressing room is Bananarama. About two decades ago, Bananarama were like Atomic Kitten, the Sugababes and Christina Aguilera all rolled into one and for some time were the biggest selling female group in pop history, with a string of memorable hit singles produced by Pete Waterman. They might not have had a hit single for a good few years – but to tonight's G-A-Y audience, and to an entire generation of pop fans, they're legends. One member of that generation is Antony from Blue, who doesn't have the slightest problem sharing a dressing room with Sarah and Keren from Bananarama because, as he points out to Keren when they get chatting over a bowl of Twiglets, "you were my first ever popstar crush."

"Oh, darling," Keren pouts back at him, "you're making me feel *terribly* old." She thinks for a bit. "Then again, I suppose I *am* terribly old."

"Well," Ant laughs, "I *was* five at the time…"

Watching the two generations of pop idols chatting in a rather grotty dressing room is fascinating. Though Bananarama openly admit that their commercial heyday is long behind them, they continue to perform at occasions like this, and are just about to sign a new record deal. "People sometimes say to us, 'Why do you bother carrying on?'," Keren says. "And I just say, well, this is the best job in the world. Why *wouldn't* I want to go out on stage and perform for thousands of people?"

As the bands mingle in the dressing room, it becomes clear that they won't be on stage until well past two o'clock, so Duncan calculates that he just has time to get to his friend Anastacia's birthday do at Rouge, have a quick drink, and make it back in time to get ready for the onstage appearance. "If you go," Johnny B points out, "you won't come back." Dunc says it'll be absolutely fine, grabs his coat and makes off in search of a cab. Simon, who's already been out this evening and is a little worse for wear, decides to give that a miss and chill in the backstage area, while Lee and Ant chat with the

Bananarama crew. On the dressing room's twin sofas, two of the band's dancers sit next to each other with a CD Walkman between them and a headphone in each ear, listening to tonight's backing track on a CD and practising their moves from a seated position; Blue's PR, Simon Jones, has also turned up by now, and Caroline is unpacking her big bag of clothes, looking for socks.

By now, Blue and the girls are getting on famously; Sarah is accusing Ant of rummaging through her handbag and telling the lads off for "crossing over into our side of the dressing room – we can't mix, you see. It's against the law." Lee is feeding Bananarama Maltesers by chucking them from across the room ("Come on, Lee, that was a *rubbish* throw!") and when Simon wanders in with his shirt off he prompts an aston-ished "Ooh, I *say*!" from the non-Blue side of the room.

Ant's getting hyped up about Blue's upcoming stageshow. "G-A-Y is always a real laugh to appear at," he says. "I still remember our first show here – nobody really knew who we were then, and Jeremy Joseph put us on the same bill as Mel B. He's always so fun and supportive to work with, that when we can we always play at G-A-Y, even though the rest of the time these days we'll be playing to audiences five times the size. It's great to be back here."

Before long it's time to get downstairs and on to the stage. As you walk closer and closer to the stage, and then finally through the heavy doors that lead to the area at the side, the wall of heat from thousands of sweaty, dancing bodies hits you almost as hard as the huge wall of noise.

The stage area is almost as rundown as the dressing room: pipes and exposed brickwork are all around, with just the occasional sign that people work here, like a bunch of plastic daffodils stuffed behind a stack of pipes. Four microphone stands are positioned neatly by the stage, each numbered, and as each boy steps up by the mixing desk they're given a number, and a mic. There's no "ONE! TWO! THREE! BOLLOCKS!" this time – in spite of all the hanging around, their entrance on the stage ends up being a little hurried – but if anything the performance in these early hours of Sunday morning is even more exciting than at Pride in the Park.

Watching from the side of the stage, Jeremy Joseph is like a proud dad. "Bands love playing at G-A-Y," he says, "because it's just so relaxed. With Blue it's often at the end of a long day of promotion or whatever, and they can have a laugh on stage and let their hair down."

Lee's letting more than his hair down – during the opening number, 'Riders', his trousers begin to ride a little low, then almost fall down completely. Intentional or not, Lee and the lads find it hilarious. Ant introduces 'All Rise' with a cheeky "If you haven't all risen already, you will do after this…", and the song's new dance break-down goes down a storm. By this point, Junior from Junior Senior is watching in the wings, too, not very convincingly disguised in a grey hooded top, punching the air along to Blue's tunes. As the band leave the stage to huge cheers from the audience, Johnny B tells them their bags are already packed and that they can run straight down to the cars waiting round the back. It's now three in the morning and the lads have an early start tomorrow – they're due to travel to Glasgow to perform at the *Live & Loud* pop show…

*   *   *

Stapleford isn't one of London's biggest airports. You'll find it in Essex, an hour or so out of London. On this Sunday afternoon most of the people here aren't travellers but sightseers fascinated by aviation and small aircraft. For about the same price as a return flight to New York you can buy a ticket for a brief spell up in the air in one of the tiny flying machines, but most people here – many of them being families dragged along by dad – are just clutching binoculars, watching the planes take off on the small runway and come into land a few minutes later.

The small cafeteria is thick with the smell of the

British day out: fried food, warm beer and wilting salad, with a bar at one end of the room and a pool table at the other. Lee is the first of the boys here this morning, zooming into the carpark in his blue Porsche and meeting Johnny B in the cafeteria. Unlike Heathrow or Gatwick there's no need to check in, go through any sort of security control, or show anyone your tickets – this afternoon's flight is an informal affair, and our pilot greets us all personally. Everyone's pleased to note he's steering clear of the bar area, and while we wait for the rest of the lads to turn up Lee challenges Johnny B to a game of pool. As he chalks up his cue, Johnny gets ready for yet another pool table victory. "You might as well get at least one shot in, Lee," he laughs, as he allows Lee to break.

Simon's next on the scene. "Y'know, I've never really understood plane spotting," he says as he watches the people watching the planes. "There are planes everywhere, especially at an airport, so where's the challenge? It's like going to Streatham station and going train spotting." He laughs. "Though pickpocket-spotting's more of a pastime down Streatham way."

Our pilot appears. "Right, lads, we can go whenever you like." He points over to our plane. Maarit, who's here with her suitcase full of make-up, hair potions and tools of the trade, looks over on to the airstrip. "*That* is our plane?" She gulps, and quite understandably: to those of us used to travelling on standard passenger planes and even jumbo jets, this is something of a shock, a twin-propeller plane whose passenger area is not much bigger than a minibus. With Dunc and Antony both here too, it's time to board the plane and inside it's truly tiny: two pairs of facing seats, one sort of bench thing, another seat near the cockpit and one more on its own at the back of the plane. Everyone starts to feel a little nervy, and Maarit reaches for her *Harry Potter* book as some sort of safety blanket.

Sadly, Lee seems intent on making Maarit's journey as uncomfortable as possible. "Thing is, right," he begins, for the benefit of those who are scared of flying in this winged cupboard, "if we crash, nobody will feel it. We'll just be squished like tomatoes before we even know it's hurting! And it's not like with a car accident where they'll come and try and save you from the wreckage – if this goes down, the only thing they're gonna be looking for is the black box!" He continues in this vein for several minutes, until Maarit decides to move seats so she's at least out of Lee's line of vision – every time the plane makes a noise, he's grabbing the seat and looking really scared, purely to freak people out.

While the band are busy talking among themselves and Maarit's head is buried in her *Harry Potter*, Johnny B recounts his most terrifying aeroplane moment. It dates back to his time with Bros, when he and the band were on a Heathrow runway, waiting to take off on a trip to Australia. "Suddenly," he says, "an announcement came over the speakers. There'd been a bomb threat. Someone had called and said there was a bomb in one of the suitcases, which had all been loaded into the storage compartment at the back of the plane."

Johnny B with his ever present mobile phone.

Lee adds a melodic edge to proceedings at Dublin's Special Olympics.

Blue at the 2003 Brits. Another good night's work for the award-winning band.

Lee kills time at the airport prior to another take-off.

Blue show their support for the Silver Clef awards, a major charity fund-raiser.

Learning from the master: Blue and Sir Elton work on their harmonies.

The flight crew needed a volunteer from the passenger section to unload all the baggage. Inevitably, it was Johnny who volunteered. Obviously it was his job to keep Bros safe, but you get the impression that he'd have volunteered whether it was his job or not. "So I got off the plane," he remembers, "and I was stood there on the runway with security. We were basically looking for a bomb. Now *that* was scary. And how did they thank me? Well, the plane took off without me! I had to sit there on the runway with all the luggage, and the plane flew off! Thanks, everyone!"

To lighten the mood somewhat Simon reveals that, in the cafeteria, he had a brief moment of clarity when all he wanted in the world was to buy a souvenir Airfix aeroplane kit and put it together on the plane. He likes the idea of toys which fly, he adds, and is thinking of buying a remote control helicopter.

"Yeah!" screams Lee. "And I could get one too! And we could crash them into each other in mid-air!" It seems it's going to be a long flight, but before we're even above the clouds, Lee's asleep in his seat, mouth open, presenting a new danger: the very real threat of some serious snoring. Fortunately, none materialises. In the seat at the back of the plane, Johnny B uncovers a large plate of complimentary sandwiches, which he proceeds to munch his way through before passing them down the plane, and the whole lot is almost sent flying when we go through the first of many pockets of turbulence. In a smaller plane the turbulence is even worse, and everything seems magnified in such a small environment, including the sound of the wheels whirring into place as we come in to land after just an hour or so in the air. Unexpectedly the landing is actually a lot smoother than in bigger planes, although we eventually grind to a halt on a special VIP runway at Glasgow airport, everyone seems quite relieved.

Today's performance will be at the *Live & Loud* festival, which is held at the National Stadium in Glasgow's Hampden Park. Last year's event was cancelled just before it was due to take place, so the

Glasgow pop audience have big expectations of today's show, and the line-up is stuffed with some of pop's biggest names. The organisers have arranged for a car to pick up the band from Glasgow Airport. On the way out, we're pulled over by a pair of scary-looking security staff. The window winds down. "You've got Blue in the car, haven't you," says one of the guards. The driver nods. "Can you get their autographs for my daughter, please?"

Lee takes this opportunity to remember his mobile phone, which has been left on the plane; we turn around and, with phone retrieved, are finally ready to make our way through Glasgow. Up the concrete steps outside the stadium, we make our way to the dressing room. All the dressing rooms here are actually corporate boxes, the glassed-off posh bits companies pay for so they can live it up during games while the normal spectators are down on the terraces. Ant drags a seat into the middle of the room, grabs a remote control, sits down, and flicks on the TV for the *EastEnders* omnibus. "I missed it during the week," he grins as Maarit begins to work on his hair and make-up – as ever, while they've got the Blue boys captive, the event organisers will be getting their money's worth and have booked in Lee, Duncan, Ant and Simon for some other bits and bobs during their time on site.

Lee's looking at the list of acts on the running order – Darius, Sugababes, Dannii Minogue, Busted. "I can't believe we're headlining above this lot," he says, suddenly struck by Blue's own enormity. After staring at the running order for some time, he sees that Blue are only due on stage for 20 minutes. He seems confused. "Simon, I thought you said we was doing the full 'One Love' tour set?"

Simon falls about laughing – he's been winding up Lee all day, pretending it's a massive show when in fact they'll only be performing five songs.

While Duncan's having his hair pulled around, one of the *Live & Loud* staff comes in with a word of warning. The boys have already been told that there are some big pyrotechnic explosions on the stage during their set

– but Darius had the same warning, says the *Live &
Loud* man, and yet he still decided to try to climb a
lighting rig at the side of the stage.

While Blue have been catching up with the events in
Albert Square, outside in the stadium Darius has almost
caused the entire event to be cancelled, and very nearly
found himself dragged offstage by the police because
of something to do with health and safety. Seems
lighting rigs, explosions and popstars don't mix too
well. "Let that be a warning," says *Live & Loud* man.
Suddenly a curtain on the other side of one of the boxes
swishes aside to reveal Kimberley from Girls Aloud. She
gives the boys a cheery wave, and motions towards the
corridor, where she meets Simon for a chinwag. After a
few minutes he's pulled away for some interviews. The
first is with local station STV, who've set up a makeshift
studio in another of the corporate boxes.

Fifteen people are milling around attending to
cameras, set requirements and big fluffy boom microphones, and when Blue arrive in the studio all hell

breaks loose: Lee decides he's going to conduct his interview sitting on a table, Duncan's spilling his plate of food on the STV sofas and the TV show's host is having difficulty reining them in. As the cameras begin to roll, though, the band begin to behave. If you count flirting outrageously with your interviewer as behaving, that is. "Anyway," Lee adds, "all the women in Scotland are really pretty." Duncan reveals that he's just walked in on Mark Owen in the toilet ("Mark just kept on singing," he says), and the interviewer throws in a curveball with a totally unexpected question about how the band's Elton John collaboration came about.

With that interview in the bag, the boys are led down the corridor for a 'meet and greet' – industry slang for meeting competition winners.

"Some bands find them boring, but I love meet and greets," Simon says. "If I had time I'd like to meet each and every one of our fans, because I really think we've got the best fans in the world. Whenever there's bad press, if you looked on the website every single person is, like, 'Leave Lee alone. Why do you keep picking on him? What's your problem? Do you fancy Lee? Are you jealous? What is it?' We see a lot of our fans as mates now, you know, they're real cheeky to us and we're cheeky back and it's a nice relationship."

Ant, meanwhile, says that he finds meet and greets a little awkward, but for the most surprising of reasons. "I get shy," he admits. "It's so weird. I go into a little shell. I hope people don't think I'm being rude... Maybe I just don't understand why everyone's making such a fuss. I mean, at the end of the day, it's only *me*!"

On this occasion the fans have entered a competition run by *Live & Loud* to design the image on the cover of the event's programme and their prize, as well as having their picture on the programme, is to meet Blue. Autographs are signed and pictures are taken, the boys congratulate the fans on their pictures, and Simon's pulled aside for a quick interview with the Forth One radio station. The whole thing takes less than five minutes.

It's now ten minutes before Blue are due on stage –
they'll be finishing the show, so it needs to be spectacular – but there's just one more thing to do before
they're allowed on the stage, and that's an interview
with *Top Of The Pops Saturday*. It's no normal interview,
though, because the interviewer is a competition winner
– 15-year-old Charlotte Hamlin from London, who
entered a competition by interviewing a member of her
family and found out last week while she was on a
school trip that she'd be spending the day at *Live &
Loud*, hanging out with popstars.

"I've interviewed loads of people today," she grins.
"Some big names so far, but I've really enjoyed meeting
Blue. I was a fan anyway – Lee's my favourite – but to
meet them and to find out that they're so nice and funny
was a really good surprise. When I was doing the interview they were really professional, and even afterwards
they chatted with me for as long as they could." Charlotte
adds that she found them quite unlike how they're
perceived as being in the press. "There are people who

think they're a bit above themselves," she muses, "but to me they seem really genuine. They've made such a good impression, I'm really glad to have met them."

With the interview in the bag and only a couple of minutes to go until stagetime, the band have to run back into the stadium and down the steps into the bottom of the stadium. The huge, 30,000-strong crowd is already waiting for the band, and because the stage is set up at the bottom of the steps with seats round the banks surrounding the stadium, several pockets of the audience can see the band running down the steps. They begin to cheer, and their cheering sets off the rest of the audience, who can sense that today's headliners are imminent.

As the 'ONE! TWO! THREE! BOLLOCKS!' chant rings around the backstage area, the stage fills with smoke and then suddenly the band are on, singing 'All Rise', 'Fly By', 'Sorry Seems To Be The Hardest Word' and 'You Make Me Wanna'. As predicted by the *Live & Loud* man earlier today, the Darius-charring pyrotechnics are pretty impressive, and you can feel the heat of the flames at the back of the stage. Combined with the smoke machine working overtime, those flames seem to send the band a little bonkers: Antony's skipping around the stage and the rest of the lads seem to be having more fun now than they have done on many of their recent live shows. Once again Blue have agreed to do another 'runner', meaning that, as the audience are still cheering, they're legging it up the concrete stadium steps and heading for the exit: the possibility of an encore dashed.

Within a minute we're in the car with the motor running, scooting out of the stadium grounds with fans running after the car. "Sometimes I think it'd be cool to just run straight out of a show and down the street," Duncan says, "with all the fans just legging it after us. It would be like the Beatles or something." He pauses, "On second thoughts, that probably wouldn't be a good idea."

On the way back to the airport, Lee is transfixed by

the many freestanding public sculptures peppered in the Glasgow landscape, most of them efforts by local artists intended to lighten the heavy mood of the city. "If I wasn't in Blue, I'd wanna be a photographer," he suddenly declares. "I wanna take pictures of art."

Duncan suggests that, instead of taking photos merely for the sake of taking photos, Lee could use his pictures as illustrations for something he's been considering for a while: collecting together those poems and musings which make up his *Book Of Shadows*, and publishing some in a book. Lee loves Dunc's idea of illustrating them with his own pictures.

"You should definitely do that book," Dunc insists. "The thing is that you always seem to be misrepresented with what you say. I think you're quite misunderstood, as a person. This'd be your ideal chance to be heard in your own words."

As we sit on the airstrip and wait for our pilot – who's been with the plane all afternoon – Maarit, who enjoyed the flight up here so little that she's actually been trying to book a train ticket down to London instead, sits uneasily in her seat grasping her *Harry Potter*. The lads, meanwhile, tuck into an array of cheeses and biscuits laid on by the pilot. Take-off is smooth and the whole journey back – apart from one pocket of turbulence which sends a salad flying all over Simon's trousers! – is a lot less bumpy than the flight up.

The boys doze, gossip about people at their record label, sing 'Happy Birthday' into a tape recorder for a fan and discuss one particular dark-haired girl in the second row at this afternoon's gig. The trip's over quickly and we find Stapleford a little quieter than this morning: the sight-seers are gone, the cafeteria is closed and all that remain are a few lonely looking aircraft, Lee's Porsche and some cabbies waiting to take Blue home.

It's been a long day, and a long summer of roadshows, gigs, parties in parks and extravaganzas. Over the next seven days the lads will be on holiday, and on the other side of that holiday they'll be stepping up their game. There's a video shoot for their comeback single and an endless trail of interviews, TV appearances and radio shows to get in the bag. There's also this autumn's massive UK tour and, most importantly, the release of their third album. This album is arguably the most important of the band's career so far and work began in London in the spring of 2003…

IN THE STUDIO

chapter three

OLYMPIC STUDIOS, BARNES, west London. Most recording studios are tucked away in gloomy backstreets, with hundreds of thousands of pounds' worth of the latest studio gadgetry hiding behind a non-appealing façade that screams 'There's nothing worth stealing in here'. Olympic's a bit different. It's a huge, plush-looking building situated right on the roadside with massive pillars holding up a doorway above which 'OLYMPIC' is carved in a massive stone tablet. Over the past few decades acts like the Beatles, the Rolling Stones, Led Zeppelin and Jimi Hendrix have all recorded here at Olympic, though today, in the airy reception with the distant clank of the studio kitchen through a lounge which blares MTV 24/7, you can just make out the sound of Blue. It's midday on a blazingly hot June day but in Studio 3, with no windows, it could be midnight in the middle of winter. It's only Ant, in jeans and a smartish blue T-shirt, in the studio so far – he's adding some vocals to a new version of Lee's stunning 'Stand Up As People'. The original had appeared on a War Child *Hope* compilation album a few months previously, but such is the nature of charity albums that it was a rushed version. This time round, there's no cutting of corners. Top flight producers Ash Howes and Martin Harrington, who've worked with the likes of Kylie, 5ive and Atomic Kitten, are at the control desk – it's separated from Ant's room by a massive window, meaning that whenever his phone rings, as it frequently does, Ant needs to tell us whether to answer or reject the call. A discarded acoustic guitar lies forlornly on the massive leather sofa.

At the moment, spotlit in the recording booth, Ant's trying to nail an ad-lib, repeating the phrase *"People* we're all equal" again, and again, and again. To our ears it was fine first take, but for Ant and the producers, whose ears are tuned to utter perfection, the conditions need to be just right. "Can I have Lee's voice turned down a bit in my headphones?" *(Mobile rings.)* "Argh! Turn it off, sorry mate…" There's talk about taking Ant's bit down an octave but, as Ant points out, "Duncan can do the low bits really well. Like, he can go *really* low. But I can try…"

In the end it's decided that he should just carry on as planned, and Ant nips out of the vocal booth to come into the studio and listen to his work. He seems pleased, and when he's listening back to the track he suddenly goes very quiet and somehow seems to lose himself in the music. During the recording process he's heard this track hundreds of times already, yet he's still finding new bits which jump out and grab his attention.

Another thing that's different about this version of 'Stand Up As People' is the fact that it'll include a huge great gospel choir at the end. Now, anyone who knows anything about pop music knows that you really can't go wrong with a gospel choir in a song and the intense, spiritual nature of 'Stand Up As People' really lends itself to such a treatment. The producers explain that the gospel section will come from the London Community Gospel Choir – who might sound like the sort of thing you'd find in a town hall, but are actually the best in the business with 22 years of experience behind them and an impressive history that includes work with some of the music industry's biggest names. They're due in the studio on Friday and by the time they've worked with the producers for a few hours, they are going to sound like the biggest, most awesome choir on the planet. "Praise the Lord!" howls Ant, before stopping abruptly. "Can't we get Whoopi Goldberg?" He's thinking of the US actress's role in the *Sister Act* films. "She'd be great." Blank faces all round. "C'mon, we've worked with Elton John, surely we can get a bit of Whoopi!" So it's decided: it's, er, still the London Community Gospel Choir.

"Job done?" asks Ant.

"Job done," says Ash.

"Wicked!" says Ant.

But the day in the studio is not over because, next door in Studio 2, there's more work to be done. Ant's looking at his watch – he's got to get home in time to get ready for his mate's party. He's anxious to get there in time, because last time the same mate threw a bash, Ant really enjoyed himself. So getting off home early is the order of the day – and Ant's working so fast that it might be possible. Ant and the producers chat about the songs the band are recording at the moment and it seems that everyone is really happy with how their work is progressing. Then it's time to get back into the studio for more work.

"The thing you have to understand," Ant explains as we walk down the corridor to Studio 2, "is that I'm always first in the studio. Rolex time works here too, y'know. And Dunc is *always* late." He laughs to himself, as if he's just dobbed his mate in. We arrive in Studio 2

– a massive room with wood-lined walls, a grand piano, and a recording booth so big there's room for a sofa, chairs and a telly at one end. The room's enormity only goes to highlight the fact that there's literally nobody there. At all. Ant decides he needs the toilet. "Is it in here?" he says, opening a door behind which is a fierce growl of machinery. "No, it's not." He sits down behind the mixing desk – which is a bit like sitting behind your teacher's desk when he's left the classroom – and pulls his cap down. Checks watch.

Ant gets on the phone. "Is Elliot there?" We're waiting for a producer called Elliot Kennedy. Over the past decade, Elliot has had a hand in some of the biggest pop acts in the world, from the Spice Girls and S Club to rockers like Bryan Adams. He's also worked with Blue on their first two albums – on 'This Temptation' on *All Rise*, and 'Supersexual' on *One Love*. First to arrive is his assistant producer, Rob.

"We came back into the studio quite soon after the second album – we didn't want to start getting laid back because there are always other bands on our cases. Plus, we had so many songs that we wanted to get going on; we're really into our writing and recording and it's important to get a good selection of tracks ready so we can pick the best for the new album."

Ant fiddles around on the studio stereo and a song starts to blare out of the speakers – a beautiful, thrusting ballad. It's called 'No Goodbyes', it's destined to make many people cry… and Ant wrote it himself. "I think when it comes to doing the lyrics, it's all about a story," he says. "All the best tunes have stories. Gone are the days of people getting into a club and having Cristal champagne – that was done in songs ages ago and people have moved on since then. I think it's all about *real* lyrics and *real* story lines. I have written about eight or nine songs for this album and I think about three or four of them are going to go on it, so I'm quite pleased about it."

Ant brings up a song called 'Guilty', which looks like it might be the first single from these recording sessions. "That also is a ballad," he says, "but I think after 'One Love' people are expecting us to come back with an uptempo track, and to be honest if you did come back with another song just like 'One Love' it would be a bit boring. Something we've really got into during the course of writing and recording this album has been the idea of progressing what people think of Blue – we've got a load of new sounds going on in the new tracks and I think it's been my favourite album so far, recording-wise."

Ant's beginning to get worried. Not only does he need to get back to his house in Hertfordshire, which is at least two hours away, but he needs to get his mate a present. "Are there any shops nearby?" he asks. Given our attempt at buying lunch over the road – where the café only had one sandwich left, which was mysteriously "not for sale" – we don't think there's much in the way of present-buying emporia on offer. "I need to get him a washbag," adds Ant, decisively. It emerges that Ant is only going to need to polish some vocals in this recording session, having practically perfected his vocals when they were last in the studio. On hearing this news, he gets the job done and quickly gets away to partake in some washbag and partying activity. Half an hour later, Elliot arrives, in denim shorts and a white polo shirt. Assistant Rob explains that the lads aren't here yet. "Bugger them!" yells Elliot, before letting out a massive, friendly laugh. He plonks his bag down on the mixing desk and blusters through to next door, where Ash and Martin are still twiddling around with 'Stand Up As People'. Ten minutes later he returns. Still no sign of the lads, so he starts unpacking his bag as Rob tests out the microphone in the recording booth. Elliot's plan today is to put the finishing touches to 'Guilty'. He's very excited about the track – previously in his career he worked with Take That, and he says that people are already talking about 'Guilty' having the same effect on Blue's career that 'Back For Good' did for Take That's.

With a bit of time to spare, Elliot whacks on the work-in-progress version of 'Guilty'. It's a stunning, classic ballad, with soaring verses and poignant lyrics about being a bit rubbish at love and not knowing what to do. The chorus – as all good ballad choruses should – goes straight for the heart: *"If it's wrong to tell the truth, what am I supposed to do, when all I want to do is speak my mind? And if it's wrong to speak my mind, I'm prepared to testify – if loving you with all my heart's a crime, then I'm guilty."*

Duncan's the first of the lads to arrive, and Elliot talks him through this afternoon's schedule. As with 'Stand Up As People', today will mainly be spent putting together some of the ad-libs that'll end up at the end of the track. "Are my original vocals good enough?" asks Dunc.

"Not really," says Elliot with a shake of the head. "They're a bit too... *singy*. We want the chorus vocals almost as if they're backing vocals." The plan, Elliot explains, is to avoid the overblown theatrics a lot of bands put into their ballads – the lyrics are simple, earnest and modest and the vocal technique must reflect this.

As they're discussing it, Simon appears through the door. His jeans are slung so low that his crisp white undercrackers are more on show than under cover, and he's brought his cousin, Dean, with him. As Dean takes a seat on one of the studio's plush leather sofas Simon gets to work with Elliot and Duncan. "Man," Simon says. "I LOVE this studio. You can just feel the *presence* in there, of all the great people who've recorded here. It's one of my favourite studios to work in, apart from my one at home – you walk in through the front door and someone like Kylie's walking out, and you just think to yourself, 'Hey, man, I'm in the business!' It's funny."

Next into the studio, it's Lee. He's buzzing with news of a date last night, but even more exciting for Lee is a CD-R he pulls out of a pocket and shoves in Elliot's face. "What's this?" Elliot asks.

"Well," Lee begins with a grin, "you know that guitar lick I was playing around with the other day?" Elliot nods – Lee's been running song ideas past him over the past couple of weeks. "Well, have a listen to this." Lee slots his CD-R into the studio's stereo system – a massive box of electronic whizzery. If you spend a lot of time in studios you begin to realise that, at the volume blasting out of the high-tech studio speakers, almost anything sounds great, but Lee's song is simply astonishing. Sure, it's a bit rough around the edges (as Lee explains, he put it together himself in his home studio), but it's a haunting, classic ballad with a massive chorus and lyrics straight from the heart. When it's over, there's silence. Elliot nods his head. "Pretty good."

Lee's beaming – as he explains later on, to receive credit for a song you've written yourself is something you can't even compare to a compliment on a song from someone else's head. "Elliot's good to work with," Lee whispers when his producer's back is turned. "He's really vibey, he really gets a feel for tracks. When I was recording 'Guilty' I got myself so worked up that I found a tear in my eye. Elliot really envelops you in this world where the song you're singing just means everything." With his confidence boosted, Lee grabs the CD from the player and scuttles next door to play it to Ash and Martin, who are still fiddling around with their own tracks.

Still here in Studio 2, it's time to get down to some more recording. Duncan's in the vocal booth, running through some of the 'Guilty' chorus. Because the chorus lyrics are quite intricate – in that they sort of repeat themselves, except don't – Dunc has difficulty getting them in the right order to begin with but when he gets into his stride the music flows easily. On the producer side of the glass, Elliot and Rob work together to get the best out of Duncan's performance. Elliot has the direct line to Duncan's head (or, at least, he flicks a switch and his voice comes through Duncan's headphones), while Rob works at a huge computer screen, choosing whether or not to save ("That one's a keeper!") or ditch Duncan's snatches of vocal.

Elliot directs Duncan really well to bring out the best in his performance, as all the most experienced and successful producers do. His tactics are subtle but effective. He gently suggests vocal inflections and small changes to the song, steering the vocals in a particular direction. At one point, he wonders out loud whether the vocals should be a little less intense. "I know," Duncan decides, "I'll do it a bit more breathy." Which is exactly what he does – and the next take is perfect.

When he comes out of the booth, Dunc talks excitedly about 'Guilty', saying it's his favourite track on the album. "Obviously I'm bound to say that because I co-wrote it," he laughs, "but I think even if my worst enemy had written it I'd still love it. There's another track called 'Taste It', which has got this great, funky bassline going through it. It reminds me a bit of Justin Timberlake's 'Rock Your Body'."

He goes on to say that one of Lee's songs, 'Breathe Easy', which is also likely to be on the album, is a personal favourite, and one of the songs he always finds himself cranking up on the stereo when he's driving. "It may seem a bit weird to listen to your own stuff when you're at home," he suddenly admits, "but to be quite honest, at the moment I'm hardly listening to anything else." Every day, he explains, he's receiving new packages in the post from the various producers who've been crafting the sound on each of the album's tracks, and in each package are slightly tweaked versions of the songs they've been recording. "It's really nice to listen to the tracks that you've done," Duncan adds. "We're proud of them. We wrote them and it's *us*. I think they're great."

Lee adds that writing songs on this third album has totally changed his approach to being a recording artist. "I always wanted to write more songs," he says as he potters around in the studio kitchen, rattling through drawers in an attempt to locate a teaspoon. "There are loads which are like 'Stand Up As People', about peace, about love and family." He finally finds a teaspoon and stirs a mug of coffee carefully. He's considering how his lyrics differ from some of the music in the charts, and concludes thoughtfully, "I haven't got the cool phrases, but still, I can express myself in different ways."

He pulls out the lyrics to a song he's written called

'Last Rose Of Summer'. "It's about my gran," he smiles, "I remember, last summer, I was in the back garden with her, and she suddenly pointed across the lawn and went, 'Ooh, look, Lee, it's the last rose of summer.' My nan's wicked – that whole generation says things like that, and they're phrases which you wouldn't catch anyone of my generation saying."

Lee's on a roll now. He talks about 'Breathe Easy' – which is about "someone special" he used to go out with. (He won't reveal the mystery girl's identity, by the way – but he reckons she'll know it's about her when she hears the song.) "When I recorded that one I really put my all into it," Lee recalls, and it's clear that while some artists get into bands so that they can perform on stage, Lee feels his spiritual home to be the recording studio. "I'll stay in a studio for eight, nine, ten hours at a time, until five in the morning. I get a massive buzz from being creative in the studio – putting different harmonies together, trying out new choruses and lyrics, scrapping things and starting again. I love it."

Duncan's own experience of the writing process has been helped along massively by working with Gary Barlow, once a member of Take That and now a songwriter who works a lot with Elliot. "We started 'Guilty' from *scratch*," Duncan says. "Gary is wicked."

In the media, Gary is often compared with Robbie Williams, who also started out in Take That. Popular perception has it that Robbie, the supposed 'underdog', is the one who has made a success of his life since the boyband split in 1997, but Duncan's not so sure. "Gary's really happy," he begins. "He's got a beautiful wife, a beautiful home, two beautiful children. Seriously, that house: it's an absolutely huge manor house, in the country. He's got 115 acres of land around him. Tennis courts, studio, everything. The guy is *laughing*. He's made an absolute fortune: he had his time in the limelight and he didn't want it any more. He'd rather take a back seat and write and be happy. He's very lucky. He's happy in himself and he's *comfortable* in himself."

Elliot's beckoning the boys back into the studio so

their time for chat is almost over, but Simon is keen to stress a point which echoes Ant's earlier comments: that the album's marking a progression of the Blue sound. Not something which'll shock fans who've grown up with the feel of *All Rise* and *One Love*, but a natural musical movement forwards. "The first album was full of great songs, the second album was full of vibe and the third album is going to have both," he predicts. "On one hand, yeah, our fans are growing up with us but on the other – well, we want to grow with the fans, too. We hope that this time round our fans are going to be behind us one hundred per cent again. All those people who've seen us over the summer, they're still there."

Duncan agrees, but he knows there's nothing which can be taken for granted. "People are anxious to see what we're going to do on our third album," he acknowledges. "A lot of people are waiting for us to slip up in a big way. Because that's what people are like: people don't like other people to do well. We've got a lot to prove. Well, I think the third album is even better than the previous ones. I'm really confident, and pleased. It's wicked."

Simon's already thinking ahead. "I'd like to see the album getting great reviews. That would be nice." He pauses for a second. "I suppose I'd like to see reviews giving us ten out of ten, but hoping for that's a bit rude, isn't it? But it would make all the hard work in the studio even more worthwhile."

BLUE'S GERMAN EXCHANGE

chapter four

BLUE AREN'T JUST MASSIVE in the UK. In Asia, for example, they've sold more albums than Eminem, and in Japan there are obsessive fans wherever the band go. Some people view Germany's pop market as being a little like that in the UK, which is why a lot of American acts like the Backstreet Boys and *NSYNC chose Germany to launch their career – even before they'd released anything in the States. Blue have already established themselves as a major pop force in Germany, where their music has broken through the language barrier and stormed the charts. "They might be different countries but everyone, no matter where they are in the world, has got the same heart," says

Lee. "Music reaches *everyone*. You can look up to a tree and even a bird is singing music."

Well, quite.

PART ONE

When you see Blue in a candid magazine feature, you catch them relaxing, off duty and off guard. But the happy go lucky atmosphere takes a lot of setting up. Over in Germany, where Blue are one of the UK's most high profile musical exports, there's been a lot of debate at the offices of *Bravo*, the country's biggest pop magazine. *Bravo*'s meetings about how to feature the band in a forthcoming issue will require a trip around the band's favourite spots in an open-topped, red London bus. In the middle of July in one of the hottest British summers in history, it will be perfect – we'll spend the day on the top deck.

With a degree of inevitability, that doesn't go quite according to plan. In fact, as the individual Blue boys pull their curtains apart on the Thursday morning, they don't see blazing sunshine at all, but a torrential rainstorm which will last all day. And yet the *Bravo* shoot will go ahead: the photographer and journalist have flown over to the country specially, and must take back something to show their editor back in Germany. The meeting takes place at 10am. We're outside the offices of the London Red Bus Company in London's Charlotte Street, and photographer Fryderyk Gabowicz is already there with Johnny B. An amiable chap in his 50s, Fryderyk has been working as a photographer for decades and is one of Germany's best known. He's photographed everyone from Michael Jackson and Paul McCartney to Britney Spears and Justin Timberlake; the only person he hasn't photographed, he says, is Elvis Presley, and he's known Johnny B for 15 years, having once worked with eighties pop super-stars Bros. Fryderyk begins, "Are we ready to do some work, then?"

Well, sort of. Upstairs in the London Red Bus

Company's third floor office, the band are kicking back: Si's sprawled on a bench with what he calls his "Beckham Walkman" (that's an iPod to anyone else), and Dunc's in the next room chatting to some secretaries. Fryderyk challenges Ant to a game of table football, and promptly wins. "You know," he confides, "in Germany, we are always better at football." Not something you'd want to say too loudly in front of the lads but, in this instance, apparently true.

Tania, the *Bravo* journalist, arrives with Helen from Virgin Records' international department. It will be up to Tania and Fryderyk to get what they need for the mag no matter how long it takes – but it's up to Helen to make sure that we're finished by 4.30pm, since there's another interview due to take place at 5pm and it'll be across town. We look out of the window. There in the street below, just about visible through the pouring rain, sits the open-topped bus, our home for the next seven hours. Nobody seems particularly excited about leaving the warm office but, clutching umbrellas and bags, the entourage begins its reluctant journey.

The veterans of many a school trip, the Blue lads know instinctively that the first action when boarding a bus of any sort is to run down the aisle and grab the back seat. Fortunately, being a double-decker bus, the ground floor is protected by a roof, but there's a massive hole for a stairwell and the rain's splashing its way down the steps. Undeterred, Simon decides to lift the mood by whipping out the blueprints to a new flat he's thinking of buying, and spends 20 minutes talking Lee through the pros and cons of property wheeler-dealership. It is, Simon correctly points out, the way forward.

"It might seem boring, but I'm looking after my daughter's future, and the future of my unborn kids, too," he says. "Not just in terms of them having some property to fall back on, but because eventually, sometime in the future, I want to be able to retire and spend some time with my family." Si goes on to explain that when he has more kids, he wants to be there when they take their first steps and say their first words. "A lot of kids know their dad, but they don't see him because he's always out at work, comes home at six in the evening, and by that point they're asleep. Then he goes to work in the morning before they're even out of bed. If you're doing the job I'm doing right now, that problem is made even worse. I want to be a good dad."

Simon's plan is simple – you buy places, then rent them out so they pay for themselves. One of his places will be the home for VS, the band he's managing and who are also signed to Innocent.

As Johnny sorts out Duncan's ticket request for the band's gig in Exeter – he wants to bring down 30 people – the bus finally chugs into action and we set off through central London in search of the boys' favourite haunts. First stop: Sloane Street, round the corner from Harrods and down the road from Harvey Nicks. This is one of London's most posh shopping locations – all the big designers have got stores down the street, but there's one particular shop which the boys have their eyes on today...

The door swings open and the Blue boys stroll in: kisses for the assistants from Simon, hugs from Duncan. Lee's already shot downstairs into the menswear section. "One of everything," Si chimes as Lee undoes carefully arranged packages. "Wow! They've got new stuff!" Lee seems particularly taken with a pair of white shoes and also picks up a pair of silver trainers. "I could probably run faster in these," he announces, and picks up a woolly jumper. "This'd be good for a girl to snuggle up to," he adds. He looks at the price tag. "I feel like *Lady & The Tramp*," he says, "except without a lady."

As Duncan and Simon try on the same full-length coat (quite a nice one too – black with white stitching, and in a duffel style), they jostle for space in front of the full-length mirror. But while the boys are shopping for real, Fryderyk is setting up a special shot in the centre of the room (it's a time consuming process, but well worth it as he's sure the shot will look superb). The shot will involve Duncan sitting on a throne – which is easy, because Duncan's here, and so is a throne, a massive gold and turquoise thing in the middle of the room. As Fryderyk informs the staff that they too will feature in the photograph, Si and Duncan are discussing who should be allowed to buy the coat they're both wearing. In the end the answer is simple: neither will buy it.

'Fred' pulls Duncan into place – he'll be sat in the throne – and Simon tries on a black wool jumper with a zip that goes horizontally from one side of his neck to the opposite shoulder. It fits perfectly, and he buys it. By the time the assistant has finished ringing up Simon's jumper, champagne has arrived for the throne photo, and Dunc's holding the glass coquettishly as the staff crowd around him, pretending to offer suits, shirts and shoes. Dunc surveys the scene. He's in one of London's poshest shops, and he's sat on a throne pretending to be royalty. After a while, he speaks. "I feel like a bit of an idiot."

"Don't worry!" chirps the photographer. "Just a few more shots! It's rock and roll!" Duncan looks rather unconvinced but in a slightly unusual outcome, Fred's 'few more shots' really *are* only a few; when most photographers say "Only a few more shots" or "One more roll of film", what they actually mean is, "We're going to be here for at least another six hours."

Before long we're finished in here and it's off to the next shop but in spite of the fact that we've only been here for half an hour, when we leave there are already two paparazzi photographers waiting outside. They've already been snapping the lads through the shop window – the pics won't be great, but if they manage to get one of a member of Blue with his pants down who's worried about quality? – but now we're outside they've got a clear shot. Perhaps surprisingly, the lads are friendly with the photographers, and Lee even stops to pose for a picture.

"The thing is," Lee explains as we continue on our way, "those boys are only doing their job, and right now

I'm doing mine. I don't expect to be in the charts and to lead the lifestyle I lead without getting some attention from the press, and I think singers who complain when they're getting their pictures in the papers are a bit naïve, really. I'm out today and OK, so I might be shopping for some clothes but at the end of the day I'm still working, so it's not an invasion of my privacy. I've posed for some pictures and they've got the shots they need. I know the paparazzi are supposed to be really unpleasant people, but you'd be surprised how often a bit of logic can help you out."

Just as Lee predicts, the paps have got their shots now and scoot off back to their respective HQs to see how they have come out, and more importantly who's wanting to buy them. One of the photographers – who's actually quite unlike the stereotypical, dirty mac image of the paps – is called Neil Mockford, and he works for a picture agency called Big Pictures. Big are one of the UK's major picture agencies – sometimes they'll send their photographers out on specific missions, and sometimes those same photographers will just chance upon picture-worthy events. Once the agencies have the pictures, they'll phone round the papers and the gossip mags, and see who's willing to pay what. Exclusive pictures can go for big money, but if there's more than one photographer on the scene the exclusive goes out of the window, so getting to the right place at the right time is vital.

As Duncan poses for photographs by the posh exterior of another favourite shop, Lee runs off down the road. Seconds later he's lost himself in the bustle of Sloane Street – perhaps into a shop, perhaps into a cab. "Lee! Don't disappear!" bellows Johnny B, but nobody's too perturbed about the disappearance – and anyway, it's too late to get him back. Five minutes later we're back on the *Bravo* funbus and there's still no sign of Lee but before long he pokes his head into the bus with a chirpy 'Awright?' and we're ready to go again. Nobody asks where Lee's been, nor does he explain himself: it's just accepted in the Blue camp that Lee, being Lee, will from time to time go AWOL, but that, like a homing pigeon, will always make his way back.

Ant wonders out loud what is the latest Lee has ever been for something, and after a while he remembers. At a gig in Birmingham, Simon and Ant had been hanging around for three hours before stagetime but Lee and Duncan were stuck in traffic and, with five minutes to go until the boys were due on stage, were still miles away. "In fact," Ant recalls, "they were still stuck in the Manchester area. In the end we had to get a helicopter to fly them to the venue – the second they came out of the car they ripped their clothes off, put their stage-clothes on and ran out on stage!"

As we chug around London in search of the quickest route to our next stop – the west London HQ of Blue's record label, Innocent – Simon whips out his blueprints again and taps his shopping bags content-edly. "I have a theory," he declares, "that whenever I get a new place, I get a new wardrobe." That's the new *contents* of a wardrobe, in case you're wondering, rather than a brand new big wooden box with doors. "And I get a new bed, and a new TV."

After 20 minutes in traffic, we're barely a five minute walk from the previous shop and the day's schedule has begun to unravel. The *Bravo* journalist and Fryderyk are beginning to look at their watches anxiously – quite apart from the fact that our surefire, sunny day has been ruined by the pouring rain, if they don't find enough locations for photographs Blue's guide to London just won't work on the page and the trip to London might have been for nothing. What they're after, they explain, are definitive London landmarks. Expensive shops and Virgin Records are all very well, but they're hardly picture postcard material and back home in Germany those locations won't mean much to *Bravo*'s teen audience. As the lads lark around at the back of the bus, things around the driver's compartment are getting heated. The duo start making some suggestions.

"Buckingham Palace?" No – they've just redone the

roundabout outside, meaning that you can't stop a massive great bus there any more.

"Big Ben?" No – it's too far away, and if we go that way the day's schedule will be thrown even further off course.

"Then we've got no story!" Fryderyk suddenly announces, a little dramatically.

Finally, *Bravo* come up with the idea of some red London buses – as good a signifier of London town as anything, and our driver comes up with a brainwave: there's a huge bus depot around the corner from Virgin HQ. It's on the way – so everyone's happy, and we set off on our journey.

Back at the front of the bus, there's a problem. Our driver's heard back from the bus depot, and we won't be able to use it for a photo shoot because of something to do with 'health and safety'. As a second-best compromise, our driver screeches to a halt outside a tube station and the band and photographer pile out for some snaps.

By this point it's the middle of the afternoon and all of London is out on its lunchbreak, and the swarm of people around the band is even more instant than with this morning's brush with the paparazzi. It's sometimes strange to watch this sort of thing unfold around a band like Blue. The band are undoubtedly one of the UK's biggest chart acts, and this is reflected in a small contingent of fans who materialise from nowhere and start snapping away with. But there's also another kind of spectator clogging up the streets and causing misery for the busy businessmen without a passing interest in popstars – people who are taking photographs not because they even like Blue themselves, but simply because everyone else is.

Fame does have that hypnotic power in large groups of people, it's as if it sends normal people totally bonkers. A good size crowd gathers at this point, and a field of video and photo mobile phones are waved in the air in the hope of getting a clear shot of the band. Thanks to being in the right place at the right time, some lucky fans can get a shot of their heart-throbs in the flesh and show their friends and relatives their snaps later. Not a bad opportunity for a star-spot on a wet day in London!

With the snaps taken, we turn to get back on our tourbus, only to find that it's disappeared off down the road to a more convenient parking spot. That's more convenient for the bus, of course – we're left with Blue having to struggle through the busy streets, with all the distractions that London has. On spotting a branch of a women's clothing store, Duncan suddenly lunges inside – it turns out he knows a girl who works there, except she's not actually working there *today*, making his detour rather pointless – while Ant stops at a news stand and decides that he wants to buy some crisps and chocolate.

Lee, meanwhile, is off again, though at least we know where he is this time – Fryderyk has dragged him in the direction of a red London phonebox, one of the few in London that has not been replaced by the rather less distinctive chrome and glass booths. There's Lee swinging on the door – snap! There's Lee pretending to make a phonecall – snap! And there's Lee running back to the bus with a photographer jogging breathlessly after him.

Back in the bus, Lee asks Johnny B if he can borrow his mobile. With all this dashing about from place to place, it's sometimes tricky to find a phone charger or top-up card. Thankfully, Johnny is always prepared for such emergencies and a phone is duly produced.

Before long we arrive at Virgin HQ. The building's a massive place, built on two sides of a London canal and linked by a bridge running between the two sections. The front entrance is by a third building, slightly smaller than the others, which is where you'll find Innocent Records, the Virgin offshoot to which Blue are signed along with acts like Atomic Kitten – but this time we go in round the back so that we can stop off at a small convenience store for some *more* snaps of Blue's London. Fryderyk gets some shots of Duncan shopping for groceries and after a few minutes we make our way into Virgin. Hundreds of people work at the label so there are plenty of facilities there, including a company gym which we find through several sets of doors, through a rehearsal room where a new, Virgin-signed singer-songwriter is running through some songs, and through another set of double doors.

Here we find Julian, another member of Blue's management team. He has a couple of CD-Rs in his hand. They're the backing tracks for the boys' sets at Pride In The Park and G-A-Y, both of which will take place in a few days' time. Because Blue tend not to simply wheel out the same, predictable set every time they play a live show, each one tends to be tailored to the event in hand, but while this is good for the fans it means that each set list, with its various interludes, segues and acappella (unaccompanied) sections, needs to be remembered and rehearsed not just by Ant, Lee, Dunc and Simon, but by the boys' dancers too. Julian hands the CD-Rs to Johnny B – it's now Johnny's responsibility to make sure the lads know the sets off by heart before they go on stage.

Once we get into the Virgin gym – it's called Bladerunner, for some reason – Simon's already there. In spite of the fact that Fryderyk's there with his camera ready, Si's wearing nothing but his boxers, but the band's relationship with this photographer is such that everyone feels totally relaxed. In Fryderyk's case, much as with the paparazzi earlier today, his job is not just knowing when to take pictures, it's knowing when *not* to take pictures, and so once again, whether for better or for worse, the world is spared photographic evidence of Simon's boxers.

By the time the pictures *are* taken, Si's pulled on a pair of black, green-striped trackie pants but his boxers are peeking slightly above, and he's on his back on a bench of weights, tattooed arms rippling with muscles and just one or two beads of sweat materialising on his temples. Next, as the camera flash strobes the action, Si's doing sit-ups as the gym instructor holds his legs before jumping up to pump some more weights. The situation may be contrived for the benefit of a photographer, but Simon's training for real.

Next up in Blue's London is a trip over the bridge to Simon's favourite London barber shop – Mo' Betta Cutz, a friendly place in a small strand of shops. By now it's 3.30pm, hardly peak time for a barber's shop, but the place is alive with a blaring sound system and lines of locals getting trims and urgent corn-row adjustments. The head barber, Paul, spies Simon and strolls out on to the street for a chat and a photo.

Right next door, Si strides into Yum Yum, a Caribbean takeaway whose walls are lined with signed photographs from the stars whose tastebuds have been satisfied over the years. One is of dadrock modster – and one of Ant's favourite musicians – Paul Weller, whose scrawled message declares Yum Yum "the best in the west". West London, one presumes, rather than the entire Western world. Though you never know. Just below his photograph is one of Blue, signed in Simon's distinctive handwriting: "To Yum

Yum – thanks for keeping my belly full." The headquarters of London's legendary Notting Hill Carnival is just around the corner, and in Yum Yum's window is a sign urging locals to order their Jamaican patties well in advance of the Carnival, as demand is likely to outstrip supply on the day. Simon takes heed of this, orders a bag (though it's for munching on right now, rather than in a few weeks), and begins tucking in as we walk back to Virgin.

As we walk over the bridge, Simon notices a familiar face – it's Marvin Humes from VS, the band Si's managing, on his way to Virgin for a meeting. Simon hasn't seen Marvin since last week, when he and the rest of VS performed together at a club in Romford. VS were doing a PA and getting their faces out there as new bands must in the months before the launch on the nation's pop media, and Simon was DJing. They stop – to the *Bravo* team's horror, for some time – to catch up on VS band news, before walking back to the label together.

When they arrive, Lee, Dunc and Ant are messing around by the canal. They've found some stepping stones linking two parts of the Virgin megaplex and are each standing on one. Suddenly, a quaint tourist canal boat called the Willowtree looms into view. Instinctively, Lee drops his jeans and moons the tourists, provoking a round of applause from a boat full of people who have not the faintest idea whose cheeks they've just witnessed.

With everyone in place, we make our way to a pub around the corner, and stop on a busy traffic island for some more shots. The cars and lorries are screeching past from all sides and it's hardly a safe place to be, which makes the events that follow even more bizarre. A car swerves up to the traffic island – mum in the front with two kids in the back – and suddenly stops. A back window opens. "It's them! It's BLUE!" chimes one of the kids. Unbelievably, the mum yells at one of the kids to get out of the car for an autograph and, with her son outside the car, promptly drives off, leaving the kids on the traffic island with us. By the time the lads have signed their fan's scrap of paper, his mum has swung a U-turn on the busy road and is waiting with the motor running on the other side of the road. "Come on! Get back in!" she hollers, and, without looking, her son runs out into the traffic to cross the road. It's all we can do to watch as the six-year-old dodges honking cars. The Blue lads are amazed – firstly that a kid will cross traffic like that for the sake of some autographs, and secondly that his mum has actually told him to do it. But there's more. As we continue on our way over the bridge – where the traffic's even worse – the same car pulls up, and once again it's on the other side of the road. The same kid jumps out with a new bit of paper and, once again, doesn't even look when he crosses the road. By the time he reaches us, he's not about to get the reception he was expecting.

"Don't you know the Green Cross Code?" Lee asks the kid. No, is the unsurprising response, so the Blue boys teach the kid how to cross the road, looking both ways, twice, before crossing. And then, just to make sure, they escort their fan back to his mother's car. Ant shakes his head. "We love our fans but don't want people to risk their lives like that!"

When we get to the pub, the idea is that Lee will pose with an empty glass. When the shot is set up, however, the sight of a premier-league popstar sat on his own, with an empty glass, in a deserted pub, looks slightly tragic, so it's agreed that he's at least allowed to have some beer in it. To Lee's disgruntlement the glass is only filled to the half-pint mark.

"That's enough," Johnny B tells the barman while Lee's sat at his seat.

"No it's not!" bellows Lee. Johnny insists that a full pint is not required, and Lee concedes that half a pint is better than nothing and he swiftly downs the lager before scooting out to the tourist bus, which has been following us down the road and patiently waiting outside the pub.

Somehow we've managed to claw back a bit of this morning's lost time, and to the *Bravo* team's visible relief there *will* be time for a trip to one of London's most well-known landmarks – Big Ben. The rain has eased slightly now so, while the bus won't be able to stop in London's busy Parliament Square, the plan is that the band will be able to get on to the top deck (without umbrellas) and have their photos taken with Big Ben in the background. After what has already been a busy day – and with more work still to come – the boys are slightly subdued on the bus as we drive into what's becoming rush hour traffic, but as we near Big Ben, Lee springs to life.

At 4.30pm, Parliament Square is near and the rest of the lads are herded up on to the top deck to perch on the front of the bus. It's a risky business as low-hanging tree branches threaten to knock them off, but the boys are immediately switched to work mode and, while posing for Fryderyk's test shots, suddenly decide that they want to be tourists because, as Ant points out, the thing about living in London is that you never actually bother to take in its impressive landmarks. And so it is that the sight of Blue having their photos taken in front of Big Ben is accompanied by the sound of Lee suddenly deciding he's Swedish. "IN MY COUNTRY, HE IS CALLED BIG SVEN!" Though less vocal, Ant seems just as happy. "It's *Lahnden*, innit?" he grins contentedly.

Because we don't get the shots we need the first time we go round Parliament Square, the driver takes us round another three times so that Fryderyk can get the killer shot – perhaps the one that'll end up on *Bravo's* cover. Everyone seems happy.

Staring up at Big Ben, Ant's in heaven. "It's weird how living and working here you don't appreciate London," he says. "You travel the world and you're amazed by the other places, but there's nothing like home. London's the best city in the world."

The boys (and Big Ben) pose for Fryderyk's camera and enjoy a top-deck view of "the best city in the world".

Preparing to join the Double Deckers at the start of their London journey.

Duncan shops till he drops during the Blue cross-London odyssey.

"Short back and sides, sir?" Simon fits in a quick trip to the barbers.

On the road and outside Virgin HQ.

Blue brave the rain at Pride In The Park.

Backstage at Party in the Park, Summer 2003.

Thousands of people turned out to see the best acts pop music has to offer at Party in the Park and Blue got the sunset time-slot.

Rehearse, rehearse and rehearse some more. There's no slacking when it comes to using on-stage time to perfect their act.

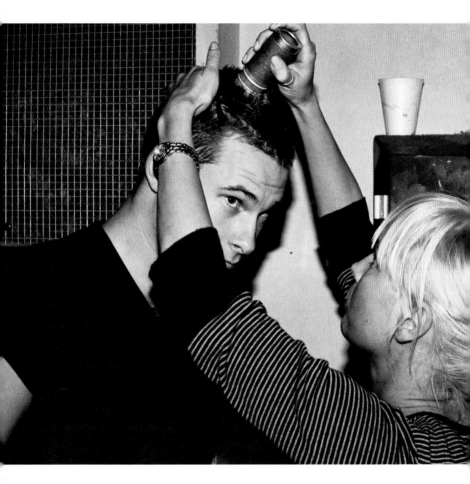

It's hair, there and everywhere as Lee and Maarit put in the hours to hone the look of their new show.

PART TWO

With the Germans having paid Blue a visit, it seems only polite to return the gesture and, a few weeks after the open-topped bus ride, the band jet to Cologne. Their German record label bigwigs have put together a gruelling schedule for the band and things aren't helped when everyone except Maarit misses their flight; the delay throws everything off by two hours. But once we're on German soil our first stop is the Cologne branch of Blue's record company, Virgin.

In London the Virgin building is in a totally different location from that of its sister label, EMI, but here at building 8a in the Köln Business Park, they're in the same big tower block, with a massive 'EMI' logo looking out over the square, hundreds of cardboard cutout Robbie Williamses hanging from the entrance hall and, most strangely of all, a 20ft, armour-plated sculpture of the HMV mascot, Nipper, guarding the doorway. (As well as being a music store, HMV was once a record label, which was part of EMI. It's all very confusing.) There are hundreds of bikes chained up outside – as there are in many European cities – and at the other side of the square dozens of German roadies are setting up the stage for a pop festival to be held here in a few days.

When the boys arrive at the building they're met by Britta Von Baer, Virgin's Head Of Press Promotion here in Germany. She's usually based in Munich – with the majority of Germany's music industry – but has flown in for this day of promotion at the Cologne office. As soon as we get out of the lift on the 8th floor the boys are working: first up is the presentation of a gold disc for 150,000 German sales of the *One Love* album. The boys pose with the disc and assorted honchos from Virgin Germany in a boardroom festooned with similar discs from other massive acts like Robbie Williams, Tina Turner, Gorillaz and – with the most discs of them all – the Beatles. Britta takes a few pictures, which later in the day she'll email over to some of Germany's music magazines, and the bigwigs disperse, leaving Blue with a table of bananas and mineral water until the first of today's journalists arrives.

"There's a lot of demand for Blue whenever they come over," Britta explains as she waits for the hordes – and she should know because, like the lads' PR representative Simon Jones back in London, she's the one who fields all the calls from journalists when they want interviews. "They've become really huge over here recently, and 'Sorry Seems To Be The Hardest Word' was a Number One. So when they do come over we really have to make the most of the time, so that everyone who needs access can get it. This time round they're launching their new material at the same time in the UK, so it looks like this might be the last visit for a while."

Britta goes on to say that, for this campaign, she's hoping to take Blue to a slightly older audience. The problem with this, she says, is that because the more 'serious' press cater for an audience who are more concerned with music than image, they're understandably reluctant to commit to covering the band until they've heard the new album – and because many of those magazines are monthlies with early deadlines, they might not even get to hear the new album before they go to press. Meaning little or no coverage. It's a tricky predicament but today the lads are dealing with the teen press, who haven't yet heard the album or even 'Guilty'. However, their track record gives everyone confidence.

The lads say hello to the media: first up is *Sugar* magazine – the German spin-off of the UK teen mag. The writer is David Holscher, a well-dressed journalist who's been working for *Sugar* for about two years. At the end of the interview he hands out felt tips and paper, and asks Blue to each draw a tree. It's part of a composite feature – those articles where lots of different popstars are asked to do the same thing – and when *Sugar* have got enough trees they'll send them all off to a psychologist to see if the trees say anything about

Blue's personalities. Suddenly, for the first time, the room falls silent as the lads get to work on their master-pieces. The finished products have varying degrees of detail but, as he compares them, David notes that none of the trees have roots. "That's interesting because roots are supposed to symbolise family," he says, prompting Ant to grab his back for some last-minute, root-shaped details to be added.

The next interview is with Julia Hagedorn, chief reporter at *Yam!* magazine. *Yam!* has very little to do with exotic vegetables – it stands for *Young And Modern* – and is a relative newcomer to the German magazine market, having launched just three years ago. It's a weekly magazine, published by the same company as the monthly pop mag *Popcorn*. During the interview, Lee stands at the conference room's white-board with a felt-tipped pen. The board is usually used for plotting out complicated marketing strategies and planning important record label business, but Lee has chosen to draw a craggy old man with a bow and arrow. He puts a lot of effort into the face – warty, wrinkled and bearded – though by the time he gets to the legs he's losing interest. As he starts on the sky he gets bored, flips the page and starts drawing Julia instead. It's a pretty good likeness, or as good as you can get with pre-school drawing implements.

The photos to accompany these interviews will take place in a few locations. The first is here in the board-room where the photographers have erected a backdrop and the lads assume what Ant calls their 'European position'; apparently all the Euro mags like Ant and Lee standing at the back, with Simon and Duncan crouching at the front. For the next shots we go down one floor to the staff cafeteria, where we find a massive cushioned sofa (in front of a massive EMI logo which will no doubt be removed by computer whizzery) on which the boys will be photographed 'relaxing'. Though as anyone who spends enough time in front of the camera will tell you, relaxing's not very easy when you're told to do it.

Once the snaps have been taken – lots of pictures of the band leaning against a metal railing, all very post-industrial – bags are packed and we make our way to the rehearsals for a performance the lads will be doing tomorrow evening. Lee asks Johnny B what song they'll be performing. "'You Make Me Wanna'," Johnny replies. "Can't we do something else?" "No, Lee. It was your last single here." We start to leave EMI via the basement car park, two floors below the building, but as soon as the elevator dings to announce our arrival, we can hear the screams. The doors slide open and a small but vocal group of fans – ten or 12 of them – appear to have infiltrated EMI security in order to present Blue with gifts, cards and kisses. One has gone to the lengths of having the same tattoos as Lee all over her back, and some of them are offering the band an opportunity to have their photo taken with their German fans.

While the lads are signing their names on various items of skin and clothing, Johnny B surveys the situation.

In his capacity as the band's security he needs an eagle-eye view of every possible situation, and it's surprising how a small group of fans can suddenly grow into a massive mob who'll end up putting their own lives, or the lives of the boys, in danger.

"The secret of being a good security person is to blend into the background," Johnny explains. "Bad security guys will be the ones who always muscle their way into a situation, using force where normally only a few words are necessary. That's where the good people are separated from the bad people. Those who go looking for trouble are just stupid, and that's why some of the people in my line of work get labelled as being bouncers. The best rule is that if you see trouble you don't go to it – you go *round* it."

No problems here, though – the impromptu fan meet is all done in five minutes and we pile into the people carrier (some fans have posted cards through a slightly open window) which whizzes us to the Kölnarena, a massive venue a few miles down the road.

On the way over, the lads chat about the new album, and Simon recalls that earlier in the week the 14-year-old daughter of one of his friends made a demand on the band. "You don't rap enough," she told Simon. "You haven't rapped since the first album. Why don't you rap more?"

It is, Simon concedes, a fair point, and he tells Lee about a short scat he's written in tribute to the problems the band have been having with the press. Talk turns to the tracks that have already been recorded, and the band muse that rather than having just one album's worth of tracks in the bag, they've got several. For a band to think this far ahead in their careers – they're yet to release their third album, remember – is almost unprecedented, and is one of the clearest signs yet that Blue have no intention of splitting up. In fact, with so many unreleased songs under their belt, even the idea of releasing three albums, then a greatest hits, and *then* splitting – a template which has plagued pop since the mid-nineties – seems unlikely.

"They'll be around for as long as they want to be around," says Johnny B. "That's the thing I've noticed with bands in the past. The moment they don't want to be doing it any more, that's when the interest slips and they stop putting in the work. I've not seen any signs of that with these boys – they're too into their music to even consider that."

The people carrier swings into the Kölnarena's backstage entrance area. By tomorrow afternoon the place will be buzzing with pop's biggest names, their sprawling entourages and enough security to match each of them one-for-one, but today it's quieter and the band walk straight into the building without even being asked who they are. Perhaps it's being with Johnny B that does the trick – he's got one of those faces which simply looks like it's meant to be places. Like all arenas of this size the backstage area is like a rabbit warren but Johnny knows exactly where he's going. Turns out he's been here many times before. "Don't forget," he reminds us, "I *have* been doing this for 20 years."

Barney from the record label is still with us, having just been chatting with the show's organisers. "Well," he explains to the Blue entourage, "there's good news, and there's bad news. The good news is that the stage looks absolutely amazing. The bad news is…" We turn a corner and are confronted with a massive concrete room full of tiny, temporary rooms; none of them have roofs, and there's a gap between the walls and the floor, making them little more than larger versions of the changing rooms you get at a swimming bath. "The bad news," Barney concludes, "is that the dressing rooms aren't up to much."

In fact, once the band are settled in for their short time here today, the dressing rooms are totally adequate, and some huge names like Ricky Martin, tATu, Shania Twain and the RZA from Wu Tang Clan will all be making do with the same arrangement. That's the thing about events like this – there are so many acts appearing that they sort of pull together and ego goes out of the window. (Well, in most cases. Fortunately there are no well-known troublemakers on tomorrow's running order.)

After settling in backstage and discussing a forthcoming gig at Exeter, the boys sit down with the German TV station RTL in a makeshift interview area stuck right in the middle of the backstage section, and the whole thing falls apart when the lads spot a pretty German fan walking past. She's the spitting image of one of Lee's exes, prompting the rest of the band to sing Usher's 'U Remind Me' to the fan. The interviewer talks the band through their new album, whether they'll be attending tonight's *Top Of The Pops* party in Cologne, what all their tattoos mean and how often they work out. It's the first interview of the day where they're not asked whether they'll be splitting up.

After the interview's finished, we all go out to take a look at the stage, where a German popstrel is rehearsing her performance. Barney was right – it's both massive and ace, with a huge runway going out into the audience and what might be the world's biggest glitter ball suspended above the people bustling with clipboards around the stage.

Most of the acts at tomorrow's event will be miming along to a backing track but because the boys will be performing 'You Make Me Wanna' with live vocals, they're going to run through the song four times to the empty arena. Places like this, which come alive when they're packed with 12,000 fans, are always strange places to be when they're virtually empty. The only people here are seasoned old technicians who've seen many stars come and go.

Nonetheless, this is an opportunity for the band, and for the show's various sound engineers, to check the boys' vocal levels and make sure everything's set up properly for tomorrow night's performance – it also means the cameramen can make a note of where the boys will be on stage, meaning that there shouldn't be any technical hitches and everything should run like clockwork when the event goes on live TV. As three of the lads fit their earpieces and check their microphones, Johnny tells Ant to tell Lee about the earpieces. Antony suddenly exclaims, "Where's Lee gone?"

The band get on the stage to find out where Lee is – he's been on the stage, ready and waiting for five minutes, occupying his time by regaling the technical staff with a fairly unique stand-up routine. Whatever humour there is in the joke is lost in the translation, and his punchlines are greeted by a silence which is hilarious in itself. So persistently he tries another. "Two cows in a field. One of them goes 'Moo'. And the other one goes, 'You git, *I* was gonna say that'." With his second gag even less well received than the first, Lee gives up on his stand-up routine, which is fortunate for many reasons – one of which is that the lads are now ready to run through 'You Make Me Wanna'.

Because the TV crews are working their way through how the running order should work, the band have to leave a gap where the crowd's applause should be, so after a roadie pretends to be a glamorous host and begs the imaginary audience to "Welcome live on stage – Blue!", the band emerge and take their spot to the paltry applause of the few stage techs who can be bothered. "Woo!" Simon woos to the pathetic response. "Thank you very much!"

The first run-through goes quite smoothly, and while the crews set up for the second rehearsal Lee challenges the boy dancers to a dance-off on stage. Inevitably, he loses, though he does have the excuse that he was being deliberately rubbish, taking his steps from Ali G's breakdancing rather than serious B-boy routines. After another run-through, the boys occupy themselves by singing the chorus to 'Guilty' (obviously the stage techs don't realise they're being given an exclusive performance of a single nobody else has yet heard), and Lee's own song 'Breathe Easy'. They also burst into a perfect rendition of Lionel Richie's classic eighties Motown anthem 'Hello', which seems more of a hit with the stagecrew.

Sometimes with pop, when older generations seem

unimpressed with current music, it's worth remem-
bering that since the fifties *every* generation has had a
music to call their own, whether it's Lionel Richie for
roadies who grew up in the eighties or Blue for those
born the decade afterwards. Fortunately, our lads can
turn their hand to any musical style and the crew seem
to lose their air of detachment and genuinely enjoy the
performance.

With everything sorted out and time approaching
TOTP partytime, the Blue entourage says cheerio to
the staff at the Kölnarena and leaves the venue to head
back to our hotel – the Cologne Hilton, which isn't far
away. As we pull out of the carpark another car begins
to follow us – it's some of the fans we met in the under-
ground carpark earlier at the big EMI building, and
they've been trailing us all day. There are more fans to
come, waiting outside the hotel. Even though the
Hilton, which is playing host to some of the German
and worldwide pop industry's biggest acts this week,
has erected some steel crush barriers outside the main

entrance there's still a scrum when the lads step out of the car.

Pop fans *en masse* can be a scary prospect for bands, but in many ways they're a welcome sight. The band stop to sign a few autographs and pose for pictures then finally make it through a set of elaborate revolving doors into the safe haven of the hotel lobby.

When the band are travelling between hotels it's important not to check in under their real names because it would be easy for a fan to phone the hotel and be put through to the room of, say, Lee Ryan – so they've developed a code to check in under a variety of names. The names change every few weeks and at the moment the boys have a set of names taken from *Only Fools And Horses*. Antony is Del Boy, Simon is Denzel, Duncan is Boycie, and Lee is lumped with Rodney. Though not quite old enough to remember the war, Johnny B gets the best name of all: Uncle Albert. Once the lads are checked in, they quickly get showered and changed and make their way out into the warm Cologne night with partying on their mind. And when Blue go out on the town, no matter what city or country they're in, a large night out is guaranteed…

*　*　*

It's Friday morning and for most of us, this is the day of the week when we can kick back, relax and get ready for the weekend. In Blue's line of work, Friday is a full-on work day like any other and it's all go.

The day's due to start at 10am with some interviews being held at the hotel, and by 9.30am there's already a familiar face in the hotel restaurant – it's Fryderyk, the *Bravo* photographer who spent the day careering around London with the band on that open-topped bus. He's just finished his breakfast of fried eggs, and is already concerned about his time with Blue this afternoon. "Their damned mobile phones!" he fumes jovially. "If I hear one Blue mobile phone ringing, I'll start yelling!" He explains, however, that in spite of some serious cellphone action on the London bus day, the pictures still turned out fine and the feature, which has already been published in Germany, was deemed a huge success.

Blue haven't yet made their way down to breakfast so Fryderyk checks everything's in order at his secret lair, a conference room he's hired at the hotel for the day's sessions. It's a good idea – with so many bands checked in at the hotel he has a captive audience and there can be no excuses about being stuck in traffic if the band turn up late. He'll be shooting Gareth Gates at 10am, then Blue later in the day at around 2pm. Outside the hotel, a hardcore group of fans remains and is gradually waking up; some of the stars appearing at tomorrow's show have been arriving during the early hours of the morning and so, it gradually emerges, have some members of the Blue crew. We go upstairs to find out how Blue are getting on and find Maarit banging on Lee's hotel room door. She's not having much luck; Lee's in the shower and can't, he will later claim a little unconvincingly, hear a thing. Downstairs, in another suite a bit like Fryderyk's, the rest of the boys are all ready for their first shoot and Johnny B's sorting out getting suits pressed by room service. Johnny eventually manages to get through to Lee on his room phone, and Lee promises he'll only be another ten minutes.

As more members of the Blue entourage arrive with their tales of last night's partying shenanigans, it starts to make sense that Lee's having trouble getting his act together this morning. The tales of his night out are many and varied, but there were certainly plenty of witnesses. Barney from Virgin is here looking bleary-eyed: he left the *Top Of The Pops* party at about 4.30am, and Lee was still there, he'd had a few drinks and was still going strong.

Britta from the Virgin Germany press office is here again today trying to making things run as smoothly as possible, and she knows that the knock-on effect of one delay is a series of delays getting ever-larger as the day progresses. To make the problem even more acute, while Duncan and Antony will be back in Germany later in the year, this is the last time the boys will be in the country together before the end of 2003, meaning that today's schedule is even more tightly packed than yesterday's. One magazine will even be asking the boys questions for their Christmas issue – an ironic state of affairs given that the UK has been in the grip of a heatwave for the past fortnight and nobody's mind is on the festive season.

While the boys get into poses for their first photo session, Dunc's mobile blips innocently from his pocket: text message received. He slides it open, clicks on the text and groans. "Oh God," he wails. "It's happening *again*." It sounds like the opening line from a dodgy horror movie sequel. "I can't believe it…" Dunc shows his mobile to Ant. "How did she get my number?" Just two weeks ago, having been plagued by semi-insane text messages from someone, Duncan had changed his mobile number. Now it seems all the hassle has been for nothing, since the same person has already, somehow, got his new number.

"What makes it even worse," Duncan suddenly realises, "is that this time round I was really careful with my number. I only gave the new one to people I work with, and my close mates. Which means that someone, that one of them…" He trails off, not wanting to confront the fact that one of the few people he still trusts in an industry where trust counts for so little, has passed his number on, or even sold it.

"Maybe it's just a wrong number," Ant offers, helpfully.

Between sessions the boys catch some of the warm Cologne sun on the hotel patio and are usually hauled back into the studio within five minutes to give another set-up, but the whole process is soon complete and there's time for lunch in the hotel restaurant. Lee decides to skip lunch and go for a snooze, and Duncan's looking a little uncomfortable. Having ordered his lunch – fillet of beef, rare – he goes off in search of the hotel medic and returns ten minutes later. Turns out he's got some sort of rash on his body and it's been aggravated by the sunlight. The doctor has given him some lotion and special shower gel. Duncan goes on to relate more about his visit, "all the time I was in the doctor's room, I kept hearing these screams from outside. All the fans were screaming for Lee. I thought he'd gone back to his room?"

He's been mooning out of his window, is the general consensus, but when Lee reappears a couple of minutes later and decides he *will* eat lunch after all, he's laden down with gifts and cards. Rather than going back to his room to doze off his hangover, he's been outside chatting with fans. He rummages through his gifts. One of them – a folder stuffed with sheets of paper – is for Simon, and includes a signed photo-graph of American R&B boyband B2K. Simon's impressed – he loved their first single, 'Bump Bump Bump'. "German fans really do their research, don't they?" he says with a smile, carefully putting the photo back into the folder, and the folder in his bag. His phone rings. "Hello? Hi man. Yeah… Really? Well… I'll get back to you." It's one of his friends, who's putting on a club night somewhere on the south coast of England in September. TV celebrity Richard Blackwood had been booked to DJ at the event but has mysteriously pulled out, leaving Si's mate with a problem. He's asked Simon to step in, he'll think about the offer today and get back to his friend tomorrow.

Lunch is soon finished – Ant smashes a glass, Dunc devours his beef – and it's immediately time for our date with Fryderyk, who's still holed up in his secret photographic lair in the hotel suite. The first thing he says when the band walk through the door is: "NO PHONES!" Fortunately he's such an affable kind of guy – bumbling around in his Elvis T-shirt, laughing and joking with the lads, that nobody seems to mind his request and the mobiles are duly turned off. Spend enough time with any band on the road and you'll know what a rare and cherished moment it is when they turn off their mobiles. While Fryderyk sets up his equipment, Duncan and Simon check their emails on the hotel computers and Lee busies himself with some paper and pencils, sketching an abstract doodle and carefully shading the edges.

With just a few hours to go until, a few miles away, the Viva Comet Awards kick off, the hotel's teeming with media and people who look like popstars. Ricky Martin, whose current 'look' appears to be modelled on that of a Bavarian hairdresser, is wafting around in reception, and many dozens of other people – who might be Germany's biggest pop acts, but it's rather difficult to tell – are clogging up the reception area. It comes as a surprise to precisely no one that the hotel bar is doing a roaring trade.

Fryderyk is going to be shooting the lads in two set-ups. The first backdrop is a blue PVC affair, in which the PVC has been messily stretched to reflect white light off its wobbles and bends; the second is a plain white backdrop with one of the boys (Ant, as it turns out) perched on a stool. Simon takes his shots with no shirt but a massive furry coat, Duncan's in a blazer and jeans while the slogan on Lee's black T-shirt – 'Rock&Roll' spelt out in spangly studs – provides Fryderyk with a catchphrase for the shoot.

Suddenly, a ringtone, that banned sound which will send Fryderyk on a Hulk-style transformation from happy-go-lucky photographer to marauding beast, chimes across the room. All eyes dart around the room, looking for the culprit. Everyone behind Fryderyk can hear it coming from Blue's direction, and Blue can hear it coming from everyone else's direction, which can mean only one thing: and after a few rings, Fryderyk reaches into his pocket and produces a mobile phone. "Hello?" The heckling from the rest of the crew is so intense that he's forced to continue his conversation outside the room but when he returns, tail between his legs, he's back into action and within minutes is cracking off some great shots. (We know they're great from his yells of "Das ist sehr gut!" and "Das ist *super!*")

He has some issues with Lee's 'photo face', though.

"Lee, don't look like somebody hurt you from the backside," he bellows, prompting everyone in the room to collapse in hysterics. The good mood isn't destined to last for long, though, because with some shots still to go the room suddenly plunges into blackness. Fred, with his lights, flashes and photographic equipment, has blown the power. Fortunately the problem is confined to the one room – though some of the person-alities milling around in the corridor look as if they got dressed in the dark anyway – and shooting resumes within five minutes.

During a break, Simon wanders over to his bag and begins rustling through his belongings. He pulls out a sleeveless CD-R and slides it into the laptop computer which is plugged in the suite's sound system. The beats start tumbling out of the speakers: unmistakably Blue, but with a fresh twist that means only one thing. It's the new material, getting an airing in (semi-) public for the first time. "'Ere, Si, I thought you said you didn't have this with you," Ant shouts. "Just remembered where I put it, didn't I," Si shrugs as he gets back in front of Fryderyk's camera. After a while, one of Fryderyk's assistants compliments Simon on the CD. "Your new work sounds great," she says.

As the shoot grinds to a halt, Johnny B returns from a food run with some thick chocolate milkshakes and a hot apple pie which Duncan somehow manages to eat instantly without burning the roof of his mouth off. Fryderyk produces his *Big Book*. It's a photo album, but a special sort of photo album in that each of the pages contains a Polaroid shot – the ones Fryderyk takes to make sure the shoots are OK – signed by the person in the photo. Many of them are hilarious-looking Euro acts whose presumably dreadful tunes will never make it to British shores, but many more are global names – Beyoncé, Britney, *NSYNC, Blue. It's an impressive book. "I've got about ten of those at home," the photographer beams. Simon adds

Blue's own inscription: "You're the man. Thanks for your patience."

There's an interview next. It's with a journalist from German newspaper *Das Bild*, who's planning to sit down with the boys in the now-deserted hotel restaurant for an interview based on word association – she says one thing, the boys spill their thoughts.

As the interview goes on, Duncan's sanity is becoming slightly limited, he finds a coffee cup, stuffs a serviette into it, sprinkles the serviette with pepper and covers the whole thing with jam. He sticks a spoon into it. "Look!" he declares. "It's a strawberry sundae!" He goes on to offer it around the table, in spite of the fact that we're all quite aware that, rather than being an ice cream sundae, it's simply a coffee cup with a serviette in it. No amount of disguising (i.e. a spoon) will convince us otherwise. Suddenly, Ant farts. "God, I'm constipated," he announces. "I need some prunes."

After the interview there's a short, 30 minute break

for the boys to freshen up in their rooms and get changed into their awards gear, then we meet in the foyer. Simon's watching a 50 Cent DVD on his portable player, with the rest of the lads crowding round behind him. As we leave through the hotel's huge spinning doors there are film crews everywhere and the crowds of fans are ten people deep – hundreds of people where less than 24 hours ago there were a dozen. No time for autographs this time: it's vital that we're at the venue on time.

As we pull into the venue and swing round into the backstage traffic system, an official-looking bloke with a moustache and a clipboard comes up and taps on our window. He asks our driver to drop Blue here so that they can walk to the entrance, where they'll be picked up and driven around to the front to walk down the red carpet for their 'official' entrance, but when it turns out that no other act on the line-up has had to do the same the driver snaps his window shut and bombs past the official, to the entrance itself, leaving the clipboard-wielding traffic man waving uselessly in the rear-view mirror. Ten minutes later the boys are doing their red carpet stuff – posing for pics and signing a few autographs – before making their way through the venue and to the dressing room area. Lee immediately takes the opportunity to take up all the seats by lying down for a snooze, so everyone else takes a wander around the backstage area.

Everyone's talking about Ricky Martin's flamboyant look, and there's much talk of Shania Twain winning her category.

Simon spots Gareth Gates and, with his 50 Cent DVD still on his mind bursts into a chorus of "Go Gary, it's ya birthday, we're gonna party like it's ya birthday". It is, of course, not his birthday at all, and Gareth responds with a slightly baffled smile.

Time for some food. Because of the thousands of people involved in the backstage area there's no posh service here – it's a serve-yourself buffet deal with much in the way of unappetising-looking food and a few salady bits here and there. The pudding – a sort of trifle, but without the cream bit – goes down a little better with the boys, and Duncan is first to polish his off.

As it gets nearer and nearer to showtime, the lads are taken through the backstage corridors and into a special room set up by the Awards bigwigs. It's split into several booths in which the media can take photographs of the event's celebrity guests and do their filmed interviews.

Suddenly a massive blue light crashes through a wall from the adjacent booth, eliciting a scream from Lee, and the rest of the boys move faster than you've ever seen them move before. There's never a dull moment! On the way out of the room, we hear a cry of "ROCK AND ROLL!" and know it can only be one man – Fryderyk, here in the backstage area with his own little set up going on.

The boys pose for a couple of pictures for 'Fred' and are just on their way out when they're accosted by two glamorous-looking, middle-aged ladies. "Who are you?" Duncan asks. "We're German housewives!" the girls chime in unison, before posing with the boys for a picture. As it turns out, one of the women is Nena – who's a bit like the German Madonna, and is treated like pop royalty in her homeland – and the other is her sister!

Back at the dressing room, one of the boys' male dancers has put on one of the *girl* dancers' costumes, and is immediately grabbed by each arm and marched around the entire backstage area by Lee and Duncan. Outside the dressing room, the show has already started broadcasting, with a wild array of pop celebrities. There's Daniel K, who came third in German *Pop Idol*, came out as bisexual, entered himself in *FHM*'s World's Most Beautiful Women campaign (and came 83rd), and tonight is wearing a black dress. There's tATu, who are missing a member tonight, meaning that only Lena is onstage. And there's the host, who looks a bit like Jamie Theakston's dad.

Before long it will be Blue's turn on stage and, in the absence of vocal coach Stevie Lange, Johnny B assumes some of her duties. He pads off to the buffet area – by this point looking as if a bomb has hit it – and returns with four cups of hot honey and water for the lads. While they're warming up their vocal cords, Alexander, the winner of German *Pop Idol*, is singing his own song on stage – the fourth *Pop Idol* entrant we've come across today. No Angels, the winners of Germany's first series of *Popstars*, are watching the performance on the backstage TV, and it suddenly hits home that the reality pop phenomenon is a massive international business. Watching the backstage crew chatting during Alexander's performance, one other thing is also obvious: that other musicians are wary of the sudden influx of ready-made popstars.

"It's a really strange time for the music industry," Duncan says. "On one hand the kids who come through these shows are really talented. I mean in the UK for example, Will Young is a really talented vocalist, and Girls Aloud have made some great pop records. But it seems like the people behind the shows are just interested in the money they can make, and the whole thing's just sucking people in then spitting them out when they're done."

With no time to ponder further the state of the world's pop business, it's time for Blue to appear on stage. As we walk through the backstage area, past the canteen (now totally obliterated) and into the wings, the lads are given their microphone packs and the dancers start limbering up. With the "ONE! TWO! THREE! BOLLOCKS!" chant out of the way they charge through the doors and on to the stage. Out at the front of the stage and deep within the German pop audience, this is a totally different arena from yesterday afternoon. Where yesterday the disinterested techies went about their business virtually oblivious to Blue's presence, right now the band get one of the biggest cheers of the ceremony

– not bad for an international act. 'You Make Me Wanna' goes down a storm and three-and-a-half minutes later the band leave the stage.

Whether they'll be back on stage again tonight remains to be seen, as the shadow of that Best International Act category still looms over the proceedings. We don't have to wait very long to find out – ten minutes later the category is announced and surprisingly to approximately two people, Shania Twain bags the prize. "Oh well," is all Ant has to say on the matter, but as the band discuss the great reception from the German audience it seems that they don't really need to win awards to prove their international appeal, they've had a great time taking part in the event, anyway.

As Nena, the 'housewife' from earlier on, is on the backstage TV collecting an award, sitting on the edge of the stage and flashing her knickers at millions of viewers, Blue collect their things together and quietly leave the venue. Lee won't be going out tonight, and the rest of the boys agree to have a quiet night in at the hotel. They're all tired and right now it seems the most sensible course of action.

PROMOTING THE SINGLE

chapter five

IT'S A SATURDAY MORNING in July. The sky's open and blue, though rain is predicted, and traffic in the swish Knightsbridge area of London is at an unexplained standstill. Our venue for this morning's meeting with Blue is the Mandarin Oriental hotel. The impressive building has an oppressively posh atmosphere – the hotel has housed everyone from Justin Timberlake to Mariah Carey, and there are various uniformed doormen guarding the big marble steps.

Stylist Caroline is already here. In fact, she's been here for hours, wrestling with clothes rails, suitcases, bags, clothes and accessories. Somewhere in Italy a fashion warehouse is looking rather empty, and here in

London, Caroline will be fitting the boys with clothes for their imminent spree of photo shoots and magazine interviews – as well as the forthcoming video, pencilled in to be shot in LA in a few weeks. "The styling for the video's going to be a bit different," Caroline explains. "'Guilty' is a ballad, but at the same time it's like an anti-ballad, so I'm gonna get them dressed so that they're looking quite rocky."

The lads arrive by various means of transport, but they're all bang on time and, in spite of the early hour, in high spirits. Ant's the first into the elevator, round the corridor and into the rooms, both booked specially for the fitting and linked by a joining doorway. He strides up to a bed, picks up a jumper and holds it against himself. "Aw, I love dressing up!" he guffaws, before making his way over to a room service trolley weighed down by assorted breakfast items. He picks at the sandwiches, then flops on to the bed. Caroline sighs: it's going to be a long few hours.

Before long the rest of the boys are in the room, too,

and Simon's down to his boxers. Caroline whips out some white T-shirts which she's customised herself with a pair of scissors, as Simon browses the clothes rails. In one room there are four rails bowing under the weight of 140 hangers, each with a different item of designer clothing hanging from it. Then there's a table, with 20 different belts, seven different pairs of sunglasses, and a vast selection of silver jewellery. There's as much again next door. Even if they're chosen, these clothes aren't the ones the boys will be wearing – they're samples sent from the designers. Anything which looks good on the lads will be put to one side, returned and sent back in the correct size.

Simon's browsing through the trousers. He tries on a black pair, and pulls a face. "This is why I never worked when I was a model!" he laughs, tugging at the loose waist. "The samples were always too big!" He's right – his upper torso is deceptively muscular, and when you get to his waist Simon's incredibly slim. Just a 30-inch waist, in fact, a measurement rare for a guy in his 20s and remembered fondly by anyone in their 30s. This morning Simon's the least bushy-tailed of the band – he was woken at 5am by a screaming sound outside his bedroom window. On swishing the curtains open he'd been greeted by a fan, who'd managed to track down his new address. She eventually stopped screaming his name, but by that point he couldn't get back to sleep. He pours himself a coffee and sits contentedly in the corner waiting for the *real* dressing up to begin.

Simon's first outfit is chosen for its classic simplicity, but there's a lot going on. There's a white bandana (model's own), black trousers, black shoes (with accidental white socks, for what Simon calls his "Michael Jackson look"), and a long black coat. Caroline perches a black, rimmed hat on Simon's head and tilts it to one side, then the other. "What's your good side, Simon?" she asks. "I can never remember."

Simon thinks for a bit. "I can't remember either," he eventually says. "I didn't even know I *had* a good side until I started in Blue."

Si's outfit is looking good already – he's one of the easiest of the lads to dress, Caroline later confides, explaining that the clothes she selects just seem to fit him. "It's like they were made for him," she says, "he's really lucky." With this outfit, though, nobody's quite happy with the trousers, which are billowing slightly around the bum area. "It looks kind of nappified," he points out, and a new pair – which look identical on the hanger, but this time fit him perfectly – are pulled on. Caroline and her assistant, Lydia, make sure a Polaroid is taken of the outfit for future reference: that's one outfit out of the way, and now all the clothes come off in anticipation of the next. This time round the bandana's still in place but there's a light grey, v-necked T-shirt involved, with some light blue jeans and a slightly preposterous, but lovely-feeling furry overcoat. To finish off the outfit, Simon's given a pair of high cowboy boots. Each of the items of clothing is nice on its own, but together... Simon looks in the mirror. "I think it's maybe a bit too much for me," he decides.

"Hmm..." muses Caroline. "It *is* a bit 1970s..."

"Hey!" Si responds, quick as a flash. "There ain't nothin' wrong with a bit of that!"

A couple of adjustments and the flash of a Polaroid later, another outfit is in the bag.

Now it's Ant's turn. His first outfit is a simple black suit with one extra detail – a leather strap around his right arm. It looks great, but Simon playfully teases Caroline, "Hey, how come I don't get a leather strap, too?" She knows that Simon is only joking and, assuming the role of an indulgent school teacher, she promises Simon that he can have a leather strap too, so long as he behaves himself. She's used to treating her boys fairly by now! Ant's on to something else, too: he's found a trilby hat and is running through his catalogue of impressions. Or, at least, the portion of the catalogue which involves wearing a trilby.

As it happens, that portion consists of just one person – an old *EastEnders* character, Frank Butcher. "Jer-NEEEEEN!" Ant bellows. "PAAAAT! RICKAAYYYYY!"

It would appear that not only is Ant's repertoire limited to Frank Butcher, but that within that impression he doesn't seem too interested in doing anything other than yelling people's names. Perhaps unsurprisingly, it's not long before he tires of entertaining the assembled Blue crew, and he puts the hat down where he found it. "Sorry about that…" He then decides that he wants to wear a tie with this outfit.

As Caroline buzzes around looking for items for Ant's next outfit, he wanders over to a rail and picks a big, furry overcoat. "Caroline! This one's brilliant!" Sadly, it's the same one Simon tried on earlier, and Ant is told to put it back on the rail. He seems a little annoyed at this, though of course Simon can't help but smile.

Ant's still fiddling with his tie as Johnny B wanders into the room. As so often, he's got his mobile phone glued to his ear; right now he's trying to pinpoint the whereabouts of a gold bracelet left by Lee in a meeting, somewhere, yesterday. Now Ant's on to a new outfit, which includes a brown suede jacket and a hat. He looks a bit like Indiana Jones, though he prefers to think of it as his "George Michael look".

Lee, who's been next door fiddling with belts, bursts into the room and launches himself on to Lydia. "Lee," Caroline drawls, once again adopting the mock-weary schoolteacher tone, "please get off Lydia." When Caroline eventually gets through to him and he rolls off, she has a powder-blue shirt and a white suit ready for him, which he pulls on while holding a cream cheese sandwich in each hand. He catches sight of himself in the mirror and begins singing songs from *Grease*.

To the sound of Lee singing 'Beauty School Dropout', Ant flicks through a copy of US *Vogue* magazine. Posh and Becks are in there as part of their big drive to break America. Immediately, Ant notices David Beckham's fingers. "Look Lee! Dave's wearing nail varnish!" he shouts. He pours himself a glass of water, while Lee scours the room for a CD player – he's just been given a CD called *The Rebirth Of Kirk Franklin* by a young gospel artist called Kirk Franklin. "I love this guy, man," he explains, giving up on the search for a CD player and reading the lyrics on the CD booklet instead.

"There's a track on this CD which is just wicked, it's called 'Blood Song', and the emotions in the song are about everything, God, love, the whole lot. Kirk's great." Lee mentions trying to get hold of Franklin for "the *Gospel* album", an album which has been mentioned in hushed tones once or twice in the past couple of weeks. "It's in its early stages," Lee admits, "but I'm chatting with the label about how to go about doing it, about how to do it *properly*. It wouldn't just be me ringing people up, it'd be really professionally managed. It might never happen. But it's one of my goals at the moment."

As Caroline moves quickly through each lad's wardrobes in this room, things are going a little more slowly next door. There we find another stylist – one whom none of the boys have ever met before – who's having to get an image of what the lads' tastes are like as she goes along.

"Well, Duncan," she says as he tugs unimpressedly at one pristine shirt, "not having met you before I'm already beginning to sense that you like your clothes to be kind of one-offs, with customised extras and bits of detail?"

"Yeah," he nods. "A little bit 'unique'."

She explains that one way of adapting the shirt to be more to Duncan's tastes would be to "cut it up a bit, then wash it in tea". While Duncan's trying on some shirts and a white suit and voicing his concern that this video might end up looking too much like 'Sorry Seems To Be The Hardest Word', Simon decides that it's time to clear off for half an hour, in order to go over the road to Harvey Nichols. But he's not shopping for clothes – frankly, after hours of trying on the newest lines in various designer labels, you'd understand him being a bit bored of clothes. "Pots and pans!" he chimes. "I'm gonna get me some new pots and pans!"

He leaves the room, leaving Duncan trying on some coats. "I look like Inspector Gadget," he says at one point, which isn't the desired look at all. Caroline sighs. "It's a nice coat," she points out, helpfully. "I think you're the only one of the boys who could carry it off…"

Dunc checks himself out in the mirror again. "Hmm… I suppose it is quite nice." He swooshes it around a bit, as one must always do with a long coat. "I'm getting to like it."

"Don't forget," Caroline adds, "you'll probably be having a wind machine in the video."

"The wind machine!" Dunc smiles. He knows that in videos, wind machines are up there with smoke machines, rain machines and strobe lighting – they just make everything look brilliant. "The wind machine will save it!" (Something the wind machine might not save, and something which hopefully will have been altered by the time he tries on this outfit for real, is the fact that he's wearing novelty cartoon socks.) Next he's pulling on another outfit – this time a grey speckled woollen hooded coat (which everyone loves) and some grey jeans with straps hanging all over the place. They look a bit like what this season's most fashionable parachutists must be wearing.

"You know what sort of a look we should be going for?" Dunc manages to say through a mouthful of room service crisps. "I really like the sleeve for *NSYNC's *'Celebrity'* album. Those clothes are really cool – there's a lot of metallic-looking clothing, but it's not so over-the-top as to look tacky or anything." He rummages through the clothing rails and finds some silvery trousers. "I like these…"

As the styling session progresses, the rails begin to look rather empty and the pile of clothes on the bed – the ones which will be worn in all the forthcoming photo shoots and videos – is turning into a mountain. The table of accessories in the middle of the room, however, has been a little neglected so far, so Ant takes pity on the sunglasses and shows them some attention. He picks up a pair. "I'm going to take these on holiday with me," he asks in such a way that he's actually stating it as fact.

"But they're samples!" shrieks Caroline. "You can't take those!"

"Aw, go on, Caz. I'll bring them back. In one piece. I'll even bring the box back." Eventually Ant's allowed to take the shades, even though everyone in the room (including Ant) knows that the chances of the shades being returned, whether in one piece or several hundred, are pretty slim. The box, of course, doesn't stand a chance.

After half an hour or so's shopping, Simon returns from Harvey Nichols's pot and pan department, but he's empty-handed. "There was too much variety," says the crestfallen Blue boy. "I didn't know what to choose, so in the end I didn't get anything." The trip hasn't been totally wasted, though – he's come back with a massive box of seafood (the slimy, tentacley sort) for Duncan, who happily chomps his way through it.

By 4.46pm Lee has gone missing, but the day has already ground to a halt. Everyone's exhausted, but the bulk of the work is done. Caroline sorts through her

Polaroids – and the pics taken on Lydia's mobile phone when the Polaroid film ran out – and seems happy with the day's work. Now it's time to carefully label all the clothes they'll be using, then get them sent back in the boys' individual sizes. Once they're back, Blue will be ready for action...

*   *   *

Records don't just end up in the top ten by accident, as much as some people would like them to. For a band like Blue – or any band in Blue's fiercely competitive field – there's a whole lot of promotion that goes into making sure people know a single's out on a particular day. Otherwise, the logic goes, how are people going to know to buy it? There's still a huge demand for access to a massive band like Blue. Everyone wants a piece of the pie – from radio stations all around the country, to magazines and newspapers. A punishing schedule of photo shoots, interviews and TV appearances is embarked upon to ensure that the profile of the band and their tracks is high.

The first step in the campaign for the first single from the new album, 'Guilty', is an interview for *Popworld* magazine. At this point, it's still a relatively new magazine; even though its launch was met with cynicism by some who thought the marketplace was already overcrowded with teen magazines, it's managed to establish its own identity by aiming for the more adult teenage audience.

The mag's first few covers have been Justin Timberlake, Avril Lavigne, Eminem and Stateside rockers Good Charlotte, meaning that Blue will be the magazine's first British cover stars. Though it's only the end of July, monthly magazines' long lead times mean that today's interview will come out at the same time as the band's new single in the Autumn, and just before the album is released. To this end the interview will be based around some candid 'in-the-studio' shots with snaps of the lads fiddling around with mixing desks, recording vocals and so on.

We meet in Hammersmith – most of London's music industry is based somewhere in the west of London, and today's recording studio destination is no exception. Ant and Duncan are already in the cab with the motor running, with make-up artist Maarit and her huge bag of accessories. "Have you been to Nomis Studios before?" she asks.

There's a few seconds' pause while the lads think where they've heard the name Nomis before. There's a flicker of recognition, then suddenly they remember: it was the first time they ever met each other, way back in the mists of pop time, long before Blue had a name, or even a proper line-up. In fact, it was at Nomis that the band first met their manager Daniel Glatman.

Antony allows his mind to wander down memory lane. "Coming to Nomis was one of the first times I met Simon," he recalls. "We got on like a house on fire. I'd known Duncan from a few years before that – we'd both been in different bands but had lost touch, so when we were both at the Blue auditions we spent ages catching up on what we'd been doing. I knew Lee, Duncan knew Lee too, and Simon had been living with Lee at the time. It all fitted together perfectly and it just sort of steamrolled from there."

The cab pulls up outside Nomis (its name is Simon backwards, in honour of ancient rock manager Simon Napier-Bell), and as Ant bursts into a spontaneous chorus of 'Memory' (from the West End musical *Cats*, fact fans), we walk up the steps to the building. "It's just like it was three years ago!" chimes an excited Lee.

Dunc storms in. "Wow," he says. "WOW! Look! Those sofas! I sat on those when I was waiting for my audition!" He acts out his first experience of Nomis. But the excitement is not to last for long. For a start, as we walk in, the band notice that there are some new offices coming off the reception area. We speak to the receptionist, and tell her we're here for the *Popworld* shoot. "The *what*?" Oh dear.

At this point, one of Blue's PR duo, Simon Jones, arrives. He's been liaising with the magazine all week –

these cover shoots are a big deal, and require a lot of organising, especially to make sure that they don't overlap with other magazines' coverage of the single and album. The publicist's job is a complicated and often thankless one – the idea is to maximise exposure for an act's releases, but every magazine wants an exclusive interview. Fortunately, in the world of magazines, 'exclusive' has various meanings. Sometimes it means the first interview anywhere; sometimes it means the only interview with one partic- ular member; sometimes it means that the magazine are the only ones to be allowed on set at a video shoot; in their efforts to provide readers with something different magazines can find some very innovative ways to provide an 'exclusive'.

But this interview is a proper exclusive – it's the boys' first interview about the build-up to the release of their third album – and it's important everything runs like clockwork. Simon gets on his mobile and speaks to Marie-Claire, the magazine's deputy editor. She's one of the people who'll be at the shoot to make sure every-thing ticks along nicely. "Where are you?" Simon asks. "We're here," says the voice on the other end of the phone. "Where are *you*?"

It turns out that, due to a misunderstanding, the shoot will actually be happening at a different recording studio, Townhouse, which is a 20 minute drive away. Twenty minutes might not sound like very much, but when the boys' slot is only three hours long and has to include interviews *and* photos, every minute counts. Before long the boys have been rounded up and they leave their Nomis memories behind as we go in search of Townhouse, which is tucked away in a maze of one-way streets and dead ends. Lee and Ant pile into the back of their stylist, Caroline's, small black car and seem oblivious to Caroline's haphazard knowledge of the London street system as they natter in the background. As we venture cautiously the wrong way up a one-way street, Lee's getting excited about next week: it'll be his first holiday in ages, and he's off to

Cyprus. He explains to Antony that he's hoping to spend some time in the UK garage mecca of Ayia Napa. Antony suddenly seems concerned. "Careful in Napa, mate," he says. "You might end up in trouble over there bruv." Ant's advice may come in handy: Ayia Napa has seen a lot of trouble over the past couple of years, and just two weeks ago rising UK hip hop star Dizzee Rascal was knifed in the area, so Ant suggests some more sedate destinations. "Go and see Aphrodite's Garden," he suggests. "Goddess of Love, innit?" Nonetheless, Lee insists that he's going to go there anyway and Ant eventually concedes that if Lee *is* going to Napa, he should give some of his cousins a call. "They'll make sure you're all right, Lee," Ant says, nodding. Whether this advice has gone in one ear and out the other remains to be seen, although Ant's words have barely left his lips before Lee has changed the topic with talk turning to plans further into the future than next week. Duncan asks how Lee's songwriting is coming along. Lee explains that he's got a meeting coming up in LA with David Foster, the songwriting genius behind songs for artists like Whitney Houston, LeAnn Rimes and Rod Stewart. In his career, Foster has won *14* Grammy Awards and Lee's understandably excited.

It might seem strange for a band whose new album is only just in the bag to be considering even longer-term options, but Duncan explains that it's merely a question of expanding your talent. "People who know us can see that we're more than boys with nice hair dancing around on stage," he says. "My upbringing has been so much more than music and, though some people seem to think it's cheesy, my time as a Redcoat at Butlins was an amazing training ground in all sorts of talents, like acting. I've been really lucky. I've been given the confidence to say, 'There's more to me than this.'."

Doesn't it seem strange, though, that the band are already thinking about what'll happen in the future? Duncan thinks not. "There are a lot of bands out there, not mentioning any names, and this is their *life*. When it finishes they're, like, 'What am I going to do now?' They don't have many goals. It's no more than, 'Well maybe I could get a solo deal', or 'Maybe I could do a bit of modelling work', or 'I might get a bit-part in a soap opera'. But there's a real lack of drive and determination. And I think that that's something we as a band *do* have, and if you take yourself seriously then when you bowl up to someone at a party and go, like, 'I'm starting a TV production company and I want you to get involved', they're going to take you seriously.

"None of us want Blue to end, and we're going to keep on going until we've got no more to offer. But we've also got lots else going on and hopefully we'll go from what we're doing now to what dreams are made of."

Eventually we find the location and pile out of the cars, up the studio's steps, and into the venue. This time, it's the right place, and the boys have been here before – to shoot the first 'Sorry Seems To Be The Hardest Word' video with Elton John. (It was the one in which Elton sported that memorable yellow tracksuit, rather than the big-budget one with everyone in black and white.) While the equipment is set up in one of the studios, MTV2 blares in the background and the band sit around in reception pondering how long it's been since their last interviews. Ant seems concerned. "Seems like, since we've been away, all the covers have been going to other bands. They've all been going to Triple 8 and Busted."

Johnny B overhears the conversation and remembers his own first taste of music industry fickleness. "Working with Bros in the 1980s was my first example of how odd the business can be," Johnny explains. "It's tough because when a group is popular they have to work so hard at maintaining that popularity. And it's work *so* hard that you really can't begin to imagine it, so after a few years they feel like they need a rest. They have one, and when they come back... the fans have moved on. It happened to Bros, and it's happened to so many bands since. If you look around today you can see that it's still happening, too."

Before long, the magazine's crew are ready for their

subjects. Because time is tight, the time they *do* have with the band has been carefully planned: there'll be two sets of group shots (one of which will end up going on the cover), then a series of individual portraits. While each of the portraits are being taken by the photographer, two of the other lads will be pulled aside by *Marie-Claire* and *Popworld*'s staff writer, Gurj Bassi, for their individual interviews. The boys are introduced to their photographer for the day, a seasoned pro by the name of Martyn Brooks. He sets to work on some individual shots of Ant in a long-necked woolly jumper pretending to sing into a microphone, while Dunc's in the next room being interviewed by Gurj.

Because it's Blue's first interview in such a long time, there's a lot of stuff to cover – most of which has been put about by the tabloid press who, in the absence of any real Blue news, have been blowing all sorts of things out of all proportion. Dunc sets the record straight on everything from girls to drunken nights out, and finds the whole thing quite therapeutic…

The big match: Blue take on the
Live & Loud audience in Glasgow's
Hampden Park. Result? Away win!

Ant plays producer…

Lee works on his vocals…

Blue go through their studio paces at the Townhouse.

Duncan gets some song-writing underway…

and Simon gets some feed-back on those all important harmonies…

(Top and left) On the set of the video for the single 'Guilty'. The shoot took place in the Czech Republic. (Below) Los Angeles, Summer 2003. The boys gear up for the new promotional photoshoot for their third album, 'Guilty'.

or at least he does until he leaves the room and is almost smacked in the face by a football which Lee has found and decided to hoof down the corridor.

Now Ant and Simon are being interviewed. Simon's interview is quite different from Duncan's – while Dunc would talk at extreme length about the Blue rumours, how they came about and why they weren't true, Simon's answers to similar questions are more hesitant and guarded. For example, when he's asked about why Blue are always photographed coming out of clubs, he answers that public interest in pop goes in cycles, explaining that Blue are at the top of that cycle right now. There's a fine line in interviews – between what the interviewer and the magazine's writers want to know (girls, gossip, what popstars look like with their kit off), and what the popstars themselves want to talk about – usually their new material. But the band are professional enough to know better than to give a bad interview, and Gurj from *Popworld*'s line of questioning is jaunty and perceptive enough not to cause any drama.

With his hand jammed into a tube of Pringles and the crisps at the bottom proving difficult to retrieve, Ant talks about doing interviews. "A good interviewer is someone who chats. It's a conversation, rather than just a string of questions. And some of the questions we still get – 'How did you get your name?', 'Tell me about the single', 'What's your favourite colour?' – are a nightmare to answer, because you've answered them so many times that there's nothing new to say. And then you get stupid questions when you know the interviewer's trying to ask you about your private parts, and you just wonder why people bother, really! It's, like, 'I'm not here to chat about the dimensions of my trouser department, I'm here to discuss my music'."

Out in the corridor, Lee's having one of his own little dramas: bored of kicking the football around in the corridor, he's paused for a moment to contemplate the fact that he's been barefoot for about half an hour and has no idea where he left his shoes. A small-scale search takes place and the footwear is eventually located in the reception area, just in time for Lee to have his pics taken. Afterwards, Gurj mentions in passing how low each of the boys' jeans are hanging today, to which Simon begins a brief but heartfelt monologue on the problems of having a bottom so high up one's body. By way of illustration he pulls his jeans up so they sit on his waist and, as he predicted, he looks quite ridiculous. Lee soon cottons on to the potential for some more outrageous behaviour: he pulls his own jeans down even lower and laughs at Gurj, "Want to see some more? Want to see some MORE?!" Fearing yet another mooning incident, Simon Jones wanders into the room and immediately tells Lee to get his clothes back on, thereby averting what might have been quite a strange portion of the *Popworld* magazine article.

With all the interviews and individual shots in the bag, the shoot is now back to running on schedule, and it's now time for the boys to have a group photo taken. This is the one that'll end up appearing on the magazine cover, and *Popworld* have a secret weapon up their sleeves: it'll be in black and white. Indie mags and more grown-up publications use black and white pictures quite a lot, but for a teen magazine, it's somewhat daring – so daring, in fact, that Martin the photographer is shooting some pics in colour too, just in case black and white looks a little *too* different. The boys assemble in formation and, unlike many of their peers, need little direction to do so – partly because they've done it so many times before, and partly because they've simply got a fairly natural grasp of what makes up a good picture.

Watching the boys assume the position is fascinating: in a split second the four lads laughing and joking around in the corridor become tensed, perfectly posed popstars. Lee's change is particularly acute – head tilted slightly down, something done with the mouth to accentuate his cheekbones; eyes narrowed and staring into some imagined (because the room's only a few feet square) distance. "Excellent!" chirps Martin, who's standing on a stepladder to get the perfect angle. "Let's take a Polaroid!" So he does.

"To start off with we were quite naïve," Lee recalls. "We'd arrive at a photo studio and we'd all be, like, 'Where do we stand? What do we do?' But that was three years ago. Nowadays we know what we need to do before we arrive – we turn up, get the clothes on, strike our poses. We don't even have to say anything to each other, it's just intuitive."

Once the Polaroid's developed, the lads break from their formation and huddle around to have a look. Everyone agrees that the shot – Blue in the foreground, assorted recording studio ephemera in the background – is a winner, capturing Blue just as they want, and emphasising the musical element of the band's new album. With lots of head-nodding, it's decided to get on with the real photo shoot which, save for the occasional interruption from Si's mobile chiming away in the background, is finished in record time. Everyone seems happy with the outcome and Lee enjoyed the experience so much that, as the other lads gather their stuff and head off for a night out on the town, he pulls Martin aside for a second and asks if he'd mind taking a few more individual shots.

It's typical that a photographer should ask for a few more pics of a band, but for it to happen the other way around, for an artist to ask the photographer, is almost unheard of. Martin happily agrees, and spend the next 20 minutes with Lee snapping some extra shots.

It's been a great start to Blue's new press campaign: quick, painless, and with results which everyone seems happy with. Then again, it's only the *start*. Over the next few months, the lads will take part in hundreds more interviews. But first, there's the small matter of shooting a video…

SHOOTING THE VIDEO

chapter six

IT'S A BRIGHT WEEKDAY morning and we're buckled up and ready to leave London's Heathrow airport behind and get the video shoot for 'Guilty' underway. Here's Ant, strapped in and chatting proudly with Duncan about the recently unveiled fact that his fiancée, Lucy, is expecting their first child. And here's the lads' personal trainer, Ali, who's terrorising the ever-present Johnny B with the strongest Bloody Mary known to mankind. And here are stylist Caroline and hair and make-up artist Maarit, also buckled in and flicking through the in-flight magazines.

We're on our way to Prague, where Blue will be shooting the video for 'Guilty'. The single's not actually due out for another couple of months, but the video is one of the key promotional tools to any single and to create the necessary buzz on this particular release the video's street-date will be Friday 12 September, when it goes out to video stations like The Box and MTV Hits.

On the plane, Ant's getting fairly excited about this, his first trip to Prague. "Does anyone know what it's like?" he asks. Well, Prague is the capital city of the Czech Republic, split in two by the River Vitava. Since the fall of Communism the Czech Republic has become hugely popular with tourists flocking to see its impressive Baroque architecture and a thriving cultural and social scene has sprung up, especially in Prague. The city also has a vibrant creative atmosphere which, combined with the fantastic scenery, makes it the ideal location for video shoots and even movie crews.

The dinner trolley rattles down the aisle. Fishcakes are on offer, as is some sort of pasta meal. Lee, leaning over the back of Johnny's seat, can't decide what he wants. "What are these fishcakes like, then?" he asks the stewardess. "Well, they're quite salty," he's told.

There's a long pause. "I'll have whatever you recommend," Lee eventually decides. He gets the fishcakes.

At the end of the short flight we clamber off the plane and go in the direction of the baggage carousel. As we wait for the bags to swing round on the carousel, the lads are spotted by some fans so they sign autographs and pose for pictures while Ant goes off in search of the toilets. We're picked up by a pair of people carriers and, as we get in, every member of the Blue party is given a goodie bag provided by the video production team. It's a bit like the kind of thing you get when you leave a birthday party, except a) we're getting this at the beginning, and b) party bags don't tend to include bottles of beer and a strange, foreign alcohol called Becherovka Carlsbad. (It's a bit difficult to tell what 'Becherovka Carlsbad' is from the label, but it's 38 per cent proof so officially counts as Proper Booze.)

It's about nine o'clock in the evening now and the journey to the hotel, through the darkened, cobbled streets of Prague, takes about 45 minutes. In the back of the car, Duncan talks to Maarit and Caroline about a lump in the very corner of his eye, just by the tear duct. He pulls down his eyelid and shows it to Maarit. Everyone in the car agrees that Duncan's suffering from some sort of stye which, as well as being uncomfortable, can get pretty big and ugly if not seen to. Everyone has their own advice on how to deal with such a lump.

"Rub a gold ring on it!" "Splash cold tea into your eye!" "Salt water!" "Heat the back of a wooden spoon and hold it in your eye socket!" In the end, Duncan takes the sensible route and phones his doctor for some tips on proper cures. He's eventually told about something called Goldeneye; he notes down the name and will buy some from a pharmacy tomorrow. Feeling a little less worried about his face exploding, Duncan settles in for the journey and explains how the video came about.

"Usually with a video, we'll send the track to a few different directors and ask them to come up with their own treatments for the song," he says. It's sometimes interesting to see how different directors interpret songs visually – and however unlikely it may seem, whenever you see a video on the TV there's *always* been a lengthy plot written in which every minor detail plays a vital part in a director's vision. "This time round," Duncan continues, "we came up with the basic idea. I remember saying to Justine who works at our management company, 'Let's not do a video that's all lovey dovey to go with the song', which would have been the obvious thing to do because it's a ballad. I said I had an image of a riot scene, with people standing up for what they believe in, playing on the *'If it's wrong to tell the truth, what am I supposed to do?'* line."

From this starting point, Duncan elaborates, it was a question of finding the right director. "I saw the showreel of this guy called Howard Greenhalgh, and he'd done a lot of work with bands like Morcheeba and Underworld, as well as a lot of commercials. He uses this amazing slow motion effect a lot, with a camera that films very, very slowly. I thought his work was fantastic, so we asked him if he'd shoot the video…"

As fate would have it, those words leave Duncan's lips just as we pull up outside the Prague Marriott, and are greeted by Howard Greenhalgh himself. Once the boys are all signed in at the hotel Howard pulls them to one side – he's set up a makeshift office and shows us some location shots on his laptop. He's tracked down a power station about an hour away which will be perfect.

"Wicked!" Lee cries, pointing at a photograph of an advanced cooling system installed underneath one of the power station's huge chimneys. It looks pretty cool. "Can I shoot my bit in there?" "It's a working power station, Lee," Howard replies, cautiously. "It's probably best if you don't."

At this point, Howard opens his folder and takes out the video treatment. They're top secret documents which are never seen by anyone outside the band and the video crew's inner circle.

Antony picks up the treatment and has a quick read through. "Bloody hell!" he says.

DAY TWO

We're up horribly early for a 7.30am meet down in the hotel reception. Ant, inevitably, is already here, raring to go, having been watching a peculiar dubbed version of ancient eighties cartoon series *He-Man* on the hotel TV.

We jump in the people-carriers and begin our journey out of the city and through winding country roads, past car parks full of logs being showered with water to stop them drying out, past freshly ploughed fields, past local kids hanging out on street corners. Ant's on the phone to Lucy back at his house.

You can see our destination, the power station, from miles away; a mass of huge chimneys and blocky-looking buildings churning smoke into the gloomy Prague air. As we pull up, we see the sign – 'Elektrana Melnik', which we presume means 'power station' – and swerve into the complex. Ant looks up at the tallest tower – hundreds of feet tall, with a flimsy ladder running from the ground right up to the top. "Let's tell

Lee he has to climb that for his shot," Ant decides.

"No," Caroline suddenly advises. "Because he will."

When we jump out of the people-carrier, we find that a film crew from MTV are already here. They're going to be covering the video shoot for a behind-the-scenes special which had originally been planned to run only on the UK's MTV, but will now go out all over Europe.

For the next couple of days the lads' base will be a large Winnebago, which has been parked up in the production area. On the outside there's a big sign saying 'THIS UNIT HAS BEEN WINTERISED'. Nobody is quite sure what this means, but once we open the door and take a peek inside it seems that the winter in question was probably the one in 1976 – the interior has been put together to the height of retro decorational fashion, while a selection of fruit and pastries on the table is being circled by two chunky flies. Ant makes his way over to the juice cartons and immediately begins playing the host, offering drinks to the crew. Ali, the boys' fitness trainer, picks up the pastries. "I think we should get rid of these anyway," he explains. "The boys aren't allowed them, and they'll only be tempted." He disposes of the pastries and promises the boys that in a few minutes he'll take them on a training exercise. "We'll go somewhere, find something, climb it and beat the crap out of each other," he promises.

But first, Ant's in charge of showing the MTV crew around the video shoot. After introducing everyone in the Winnebago to the MTV audience, he takes the crew out around the site. "And this," he declares, "this is a power station." He has a look around. "We might as well have done it in Battersea!" (Battersea Power Station is where the video for 'If U Come Back' was shot.)

Back in the Winnebago, Lee's having some sort of existential crisis over the fact that everybody thinks he looks like Stifler from *American Pie* ("I don't, do I?" he asks the room, to be answered by an ominous silence), and Duncan emerges from the bedroom with massive clamps over his eyes. He's still having problems with the stye from last night, and Maarit is helping to minimise the swelling, but his tiredness isn't helping – he was awake until 3am, not partying or making the most of his posh hotel room but lying in bed, terrified to fall asleep in case he woke up with a lump the size of a football having grown on his face. "In the end," he explains, "I managed to convince myself that if I *did* have a rubbish eye, I could wear an eyepatch for the entire video shoot. Like a pirate, or something." Fortunately for Duncan's burgeoning role as a pop style icon, the swelling's gone down considerably, so the Captain Hook 'look' can be postponed indefinitely.

The Blue flatulence routine rears its head once again at 11.15am when Lee, having his hair pulled into position by Maarit, lets rip and the long-suffering hairlady finds it necessary to blow the fumes away using her hairdryer, but the worst of it is wafted away when the door opens. In walks Carole, Blue's video commissioner, brandishing a CD. It contains three tracks. The first track is 'Guilty'. So, in fact, are the other two – but track two is at one and a half times the speed of the original, and track three is at double speed. When the boys are filming later today they'll be lip-synching to all three versions.

Director Howard talks us through the reasons for this. "Normal film shoots at 24 frames per second," he begins. "But we're going to be shooting at a *thousand* frames per second, which means that when you play it back at 24 frames a second everything's in extreme slow motion. But because Blue will have been singing the song at double speed in real life, when the film is slowed down they'll match the normal song, but every-thing around them will be moving in slow motion. It's a stunning technique – drop a dime and it would take 40 seconds to hit the floor."

We decide to listen to the CD. After a false start in which the entire band have a go at working the Winnebago's CD player, the fast mixes are blaring out. As it happens they both sound pretty good – as Ant points out, "it's like a garage remix, innit?"

Later on, Ant chooses a quiet moment to reprise his Frank Butcher impression from the clothes fitting last month. He appears from the bedroom wearing Simon's hat. "Jer-neeeen!" he bellows. "PAT!" He's amusing himself, at very least.

Lee and Duncan return from their training session, panting and covered in sweat. "I love doing it bare knuckle," Lee says, holding up a moist fist. It turns out Ali has built a sort of makeshift gym out in the power station wasteland, with iron girders taking the place of a set of weights. Dunc's managed to hit himself on the head during the session and is just waiting for a bruise to appear. Something else is happening outside, too – some spots of rain. This is not part of today's plan – apparently it's the first time it's rained in Prague for three and a half months – but the show will go on and the shoot has to begin on schedule or else it will all end up overrunning and incurring additional costs .

"It's going to be one of those videos," Duncan sighs as he trims his beard. He peers at himself in the mirror and begins pulling his eyebrow to one side. "Do you think," he begins, "I should shave a line in my right eyebrow?"

There's an audible intake of breath. "No!" shrieks Maarit, scanning the room for razors in case Duncan suddenly gets the urge. "But why not?" Dunc asks, innocently. "It's been a bit done to death," says someone from Virgin.

With shooting due to begin in 45 minutes, Duncan's eye is proving a cause for concern, even with his hair brushed strategically over the problem zone. Johnny B is dispatched to a local pharmacy – in so far as anything can be considered 'local' to this remote power station – in order to purchase a tube of something called chloramycetine. He writes it down on a piece of paper but as soon as he's out of earshot the lads start to wonder whether their tour manager, with his broad east London accent, will be able to break the language barrier.

During all this time, Simon has been sprawled on the Winnebago sofa, dead to the world. Nothing has woken him – not Lee's farting, or Maarit's fart-induced shrieking, or an MTV crew clanking around the room. He comes around of his own accord and finds the MTV camera buzzing around. He puts on his chain and explains to the camera that he's gradually wearing heavier and heavier chains, in an attempt "to build my neck up". Nobody seems in the slightest bit convinced. When Duncan threatens to introduce the whole Blue entourage to MTV viewers there's a sudden flurry as everyone on the bus bolts for the door, but a few unlucky ones are caught in the camera's gaze. "It's always a relief to work with UK bands like Blue," the MTV girl says later. "In the States they're so paranoid about security that you can't even film the security guards. With this lot you always get really good access."

Johnny B appears in the doorway, empty-handed after his trip to the pharmacy as the medication Duncan required was prescription-only. "Come on boys," he booms, "you're due on set!"

The production crew have been here in Prague for the past couple of days sorting out various locations around the power station. The base – a couple of minutes' walk from the Winnebago, and the place where most of the action will be filmed – is a large tarmacked area around the size of a decent-sized supermarket car park, with massive buildings all around it. There's a helicopter parked a couple of hundred yards away and the local fire crew are all here with their fire engine, ready for action should they be required.

Video director Howard comes over and reintroduces himself to the boys, then talks them through what'll be required for the first shot. The two 'sides' in the video – that's the truth and lies element – are both in this shot. The grey mob are in a grey car, the black mob in a black car. (The rest of the extras have their grey and black clothes on, too – and, like the guinea pigs in some strange sort of psychological experiment, have inadvertently grouped off in their respective colours.) Both cars will be circling in the tarmacked area, and the boys will walk through the shot with the cars whizzing past them. Blue nod in acknowledgement, and take their places.

The volume of the 'Guilty' CD – at 1.5 times its normal speed – is cranked up and the cameras are rolling, filming the same scene seven or eight times before Howard is certain they've got a good shot in the can. Afterwards, because they've been shooting some of the cameras in digital, the footage is played back on a monitor and the lads crowd round to see how they look. They look fine, is the consensus opinion – and Dunc's wonky eye is not in view. Sighs of relief all round, then the boys return to their positions to do the same shot *again* – this time in close up. Johnny produces a disposable camera from his pocket and begins snapping away. He's been given yet another role for the shoot – official photographer, with pictures due to appear in some European pop magazines when the single comes out.

With the close-ups finished, it's lunchtime, and the lads pile in to grab some food. One of the menu options is a kind of European version of bangers and mash. Duncan's verdict on the sausage and spud lunch? "It's quite nice, actually."

As the lads finish lunch, the sun comes out,

meaning that the weather is now good enough for some helicopter action. Caroline takes this opportunity to reflect on how well today's shoot is going compared with a photo shoot she and the boys endured in LA the previous week. It had originally been the plan to shoot this video out there, too, but in the end the trip was cut short by a few days and scaled down to include only stills photos. A good move, as it turned out.

"Oh, God," she begins, as memories of the trip start flooding back. "Well basically, I'd worked so hard on this project right from the start. From before we even had that fitting day at the Mandarin Oriental hotel. I'd been saying, 'Simon, I'm going to make you into movie stars.' I did all these mood boards. I took Polaroids. I got my brother in on it because my brother models all the boys' clothes to test them out. The shoot in LA was the culmination of something like six months' work. So, we arrived at the airport on that side of the trip, and we were waiting for the luggage to come on to the carousel. And we were waiting. And waiting..." She begins to scream and hold her head in her hands. "And at the time I wasn't panicked. I was like 'Cool, yeah, they'll arrive tomorrow'. Except they didn't. No one could talk to me. Nobody. I was just livid. All I knew was that for some unknown, ungodly reason, there were no clothes for the photo shoot."

Caroline advises that there was a valuable amount of clothing in those bags – and for days, nobody knew where it was. Eventually the clothes turned up in one piece and Caroline's worst nightmare was averted, though to this day nobody is quite sure what sort of journey the clothes had in those intervening days. The rest of the shoot went smoothly – it was in a special set at the legendary Paramount film studios and the band whiled away their hours racing each other round the set in golf carts – but Caroline pauses to think about what she might have done if the clothes had totally disappeared, or if she only had a few hundred quid to get the band dressed.

"Well I would cry, for a start," she laughs. "And when

I'd finished crying, I'd just go down to the high street, and I'd just buy them all the best bargains I could find."

Back in the Winnebago, Duncan and Lee are both taking the opportunity to catch up on some sleep, while Ant and Simon are chatting about fatherhood. Suddenly Simon jumps up and disappears into Maarit's bedroom-cum-wardrobe, reappearing a moment later with a needle and thread. He holds the thread at one end and tells Ant to hold his hand out. The need is dangled over Ant's hand and Simon explains that if the needle swings backwards and forwards Ant can expect a boy; if it swings in a circle, Ant will have a girl. It swings in a circle. "It's going to be a girl!" Simon declares, though there's a bit of confusion over whether the test shouldn't really be done over the mother's hand. Still, Simon seems pleased enough with his prediction and already has a bond with the unborn child – Lucy is expected to give birth on Simon's own birthday. "That'd make my baby an Aries," he smiles. "It'll be a good kid – Aries people have got *fire* in them."

Lunch and baby-gender-prediction over, it's time for

the boys to get back on set. When we arrive, the extras are separated into greys and black, and are standing on either side of the set. It looks a bit like a recreation of *Braveheart*. One of the production crew explains the next scene to the band. "The theme for this shot is that it's chaos," he says, "and I think it probably will be. You'll be in the middle, and the two sides will run across the shot, fighting past each other, knocking you out of the way."

There's no time to contemplate how the boys will look – as over on the other side of the power station, a helicopter is whirring into action. Once it's in the air the cameras begin to roll and the two sides of rioters begin charging at each other. The helicopter swoops above our heads, churning up the dust and rubbish on the ground and creating a cloud of debris, with Blue right at the centre. As predicted, it's chaos, but it looks amazing. Flags billow in the gale, smoke canisters explode into action, extras smash into each other, are knocked to the ground, and pick themselves up to do battle again.

The shot is captured several times, and in most instances Lee finds himself knocked to the ground, though this is probably because he keeps taunting the extras to "run straight into me and give me a right kicking". Amid the riot, the less provocative Duncan also manages to get himself smacked on the nose.

As the helicopter touches down once more and its blades spin to a slow halt, everyone in the crew realises that they're covered in dirt. God only knows what it contains – nobody in the band is quite sure what sort of dirt you get around Prague power stations – but with grass and debris in our hair, the result is an unusual scarecrow look. This evening, when we get back to the hotel and freshen up, every one of us will step out of the shower to find a tub full of dirt.

As the cameras get into position for the next shot, Duncan chats with the rest of the boys about how the video is going. He smiles through the pain of his bumped nose. "It's very, very chilled out," he decides, "which is nice. I like chilled out shoots. There's nothing worse than a video shoot where the director is difficult and being really finicky about everything. Howard is really chilled, a really nice guy. He's a good Halifax lad, you see."

For the boys, one of their most memorable shoots to date has been for 'You Make Me Wanna'. Simon has particularly fond memories of the video. "Well you see the thing is," he begins, allowing a broad grin to spread across his face, "I was the one who cast all the girls for the video. Before the shoot, the director came up to me and he was like, 'I've got this picture of a girl, she's the one I picture being with you on the video.' I looked at it and I was like, 'No offence, mate, but she's not the type of girl I go for. That's not the type of girl I'd be singing *"You make me wanna call you in the middle of the night"* to.' I wanted the video to be as near to reality as possible, and the director invited me to the casting session the next day. I went along and I stood in the background, watching all these girls…" Simon explains that as he was assessing the girls' suitability for the shoot, in a purely professional capacity, he began thinking about his fans and how they might get the wrong idea. Perhaps, he thought, if the 'girlfriend' in the video seemed so realistic, fans might think she actually *was* his girlfriend. "But then I thought, 'You know what? They won't mind'. So I chose the woman of my dreams!"

Simon and the girl ended up "really, really good mates. To look at, she might have been the best thing since sliced bread – and I'll tell you what, the video doesn't do her justice – but what I really found magnetic about her was how intelligent she was. She knew exactly what she was talking about. I know it's a cliché, but good looks wear off. Actually, perhaps her looks will *never* wear off. But you know what I mean. She wasn't one of these pretty girls who just smiles. She made me laugh and she made me be myself and in the end we ended up getting on like a house on fire."

The rest of the band and crew will remember the 'You Make Me Wanna' video for altogether less glamorous reasons, all attributable to the fact that some of the scenes were filmed on a boat. Boats can be risky vessels at the best of times and when you're out on one all day, the rolling motion can get too much. On day one of the shoot Caroline was left stranded on a desert island while the rest of the crew took it in turns to be sick off the back of the boat; on the second day, everyone was so knocked out by anti-seasickness pills that they kept falling asleep.

"At least," Antony announces, "it made a change from walking down a street. For some reason that's what we always end up doing in videos. 'Oh look – it's Blue looking moody and walking down a street!' 'Oh look – it's Blue looking moody and walking down a slightly different street!' At least on that one you got us looking slightly unwell on a boat."

They briefly reminisce over some of their other videos, there's amused recollections of the 'All Rise' shoot – the band's first – in which, through 2003 eyes, the boys appear almost unrecognisable.

Before the next portion of the video is recorded the lads record a couple of idents – of the "Hi, we're Blue" variety – for the MTV film crew. The snippets will be used on the *TRL* show, which is due to launch in a few weeks. In America, the *TRL* (*Total Request Live*) slot is one of the jewels in MTV's crown, and the daily rundown of the videos and songs which have been most requested by the channel's viewers is a huge opportunity for bands to help create a buzz about their songs before they're even in the shops. The signs are already looking good for 'Guilty', though, because one of the idents they're asked to record is "Hi, we're Blue, and thanks for making our video Number One". With the shots in the can, Simon darts forwards, picks up the MTV girl in a fireman's lift and trots off into the distance with her over his shoulder, slapping her bum as he goes. He runs round a corner, and all that is left of the filmcrew's frontwoman is the distant screaming of "Si! Si! Put me down, you fool!" Eventually the hollering subsides and Simon reappears from around the corner with a grin on his face.

The lads return to the set for one more shot – close-ups of some chorus moments – and by 8pm they're finished. Some video shoots are crammed into one day, meaning that they'll eventually wrap in the early hours of the morning, but because this one's being filmed over two days the boys get the luxury of an early finish.

Back at the hotel, Blue are refreshed and changed – and free of the helicopter-strewn gunk – by 10pm, so we meet in the hotel restaurant for a late dinner. It's a lively atmosphere, with beer and wine flowing freely as the band unwind, talking rubbish into the early hours but politely declining some of the locals' invitation to join them at a local casino. After all, tomorrow is another early start – and we're only halfway through the video shoot.

DAY THREE

It's 7.30am. As ever, Ant is early, beating not just the band but the entire entourage down to reception. He's clutching an envelope full of paper, the contents of which are never revealed, and will tell anyone who'll listen what he watched on TV last night. Not another episode of dubbed *He-Man*, but *8-Mile* on the hotel pay-per-view. It's the first time he's seen it, and he's blown away. By 7.45am, everyone's down here except Caroline and Maarit, who appear in due course. The sun's out today, which makes a pleasant change from yesterday's moody weather, and on the way to the power station Ant and Simon discuss what the video people have in store for today's shots. From the riots and helicopters yesterday, things are due to step up a gear. Ant will begin the day by running through fire, while Simon's stunt will involve water. "They've got it the wrong way round," Si grumps good-naturedly. "I'm a fire sign and Ant's a water sign. Oh well."

As we pass the fields of corn – the proper, tall corn plants like in the films – Maarit discusses Duncan's rollcall of facial disfigurements. On top of the still-present lump on his eye, his nose has gone a bit wonky after being whacked during yesterday's riot scene. "Thing is," Ant helpfully offers, "these things always come in threes." Maarit looks worried, and Ant decides to wind her up even further by calling her Abba, after the seventies Swedish supergroup... It'll be a while before we see if anything else has happened to Duncan, though, because for the second night in a row he's had difficulty sleeping and will be using the couple of hours before his first shot to try to get an extra few winks, even if the requisite forty seems a little optimistic. During the journey, as the huge power station looms into view on the horizon, we pass a branch of Tesco, which is nice.

Arriving on the site to the smell of the catering van's slightly burnt bacon breakfast, Simon goes off to have a look around today's set, while Ant is given the duty of chatting to a film crew from GM:TV, who will be doing today what MTV were doing yesterday. Except MTV are due here today too, meaning there are two extra film units vying for time with the lads. Ant begins his first piece to camera: "Hi, I'm Ant from Blue and I'm on my own. No, we haven't split up – the rest of the boys are still in bed..."

At 10am, Ant's ready for his dice with death. Well, that's how it'll appear in the video at least, but while he's due to be running around with lots of fire all over the place the dangerous bit will really be suggested by strategically placed cameras; he's pretty safe. The plan is this: two massive, 40-foot square black sheets are held up by scaffolding, one set slightly back from the other. Both will be doused in something flammable and set on fire, and Ant will run, with a dozen or so of the extras, between the two, turning the corner and sprinting towards the camera. As he does this, bits of black sheet will float off into the air, and a firecannon will blast flames in his path. For obvious reasons, there's a no-smoking policy on this part of the set, and the local fire crew are here again as an extra safety precaution.

The MTV crew observe Ant's hair. "Lots of hairspray today, Ant," one of them says. "Hairspray and fire are a good combination, aren't they?"

"Yeah, thanks mate," Ant laughs. "Thanks for the

confidence. Remind me to come round your house if I ever need cheering up!"

After a 'no flame rehearsal' Ant's ready to do the shot for real. The black sheets are doused in fuel – you can smell it in the air, even at some distance – and Director Howard has a word with Ant. "Now, it might seem a little undramatic when you're doing it, but it'll look great when it's slowed down," he says, though when the wind eventually decides to blow in the right direction and he yells 'Action!' and the flames explode everywhere, it looks quite dramatic enough, thank you very much. Ant escapes the shot unsinged, though one of the extras, who's been running around with a burning flag, loses the hair on the back of his hand. It's an impressive sequence and Ant seems genuinely exhilarated by the experience, though most of the Blue entourage have missed his moment of glory due to a persistent Czech wasp sending everyone running for cover.

Someone else who missed the escapade was Lee, who's just turned up in a car with Duncan. Like Simon,

Lee's individual scene will involve water. "This scene," he tells the GMTV crew, "is where I lose my pants in the swimming pool, and then I dramatically put them back on again." (It's nothing of the sort.)

We walk around a corner of the power station. Where yesterday's riots'n'helicopters scene took place there is now a huge pool of water – about 40 feet square and four inches deep – whose housing has been fashioned from rocks and black binbag plastic, as if Charlie Dimmock had been asked to make a water feature in a warzone. Wind machines are at the ready, as are the extras, dressed once again in their grey and black boilersuits, separated on each side of the pool. When the cameras – covered in splash-proof binbags – begin to roll, Lee will lipsynch 'Guilty' while standing in the middle of the pool, and both groups of extras will run across the pool. There will be a lot of splashing.

The fire crew are on standby once again, this time to make sure the pool is kept topped up with water, and seemingly from nowhere vast plates of doughnuts have appeared to keep the crew's energy levels up. The cameras roll and with a degree of inevitability Lee ends up soaked from head to foot, so makes his way back to the Winnebago to change into new clothes while his wet ones are hung up in the sun to dry. When he gets there he discovers Ant and Caroline yelling at each other – Ant has proposed a hip hop general knowledge quiz and things have become rather heated.

Lee sits down to dry off in a loose white T-shirt and grey trackie bottoms, munch his way through lunch – salmon and salad is the popular choice today – and watch his *Incredible Hulk* DVD.

The GMTV crew have got all the shots they need and bid us all a farewell, and while the rest of the crew tuck into their lunches Johnny decides to go off to the shop and buy some supplies. As he walks off the site, he spots Lee's clothes – which have dried on the side facing the sun – and turns them over so the other side can dry. It's a small gesture which could easily go unnoted, but it's the cumulative effect of all Johnny's small gestures that makes him such a vital cog in the Blue machine. (As it happens, someone does notice the clothes having been turned. When Caroline thanks Johnny later on and his response is "How did you know it was me?', her answer is simple: "Well, nobody else would have bothered, would they?")

Johnny B's Five Golden Rules

1. Be as punctual as you possibly can. Even if you're just five minutes late for something you find yourself playing catch-up all day.

2. Never lie, because it'll come round and slap you in the face.

3. Always be polite and courteous. Nobody's going to give you any respect if you don't give some out too.

4. When you're wrong, admit you're wrong.

5. Always be true to yourself.

After lunch, Duncan has been on set for an hour (his eye and nose are looking better, to much relief) and he assumes the position for his own solo shot. This one's quite complex – on the concreted area, a stuntman is standing motionless with a water cannon shooting a massive stream of water at his back, which in turn sends the water spraying in arcs across the scene, blown all over the shop by massive wind machines. Behind him, Duncan stands two paces in front of a wall of rioters and as Howard yells 'Action' once again Dunc runs towards the camera, leading the army through the waterspray. Like Lee, he gets absolutely soaked – and gets a mouthful of water, to boot.

Simon is watching from behind the camera.

Ant's phone rings. It's Lucy calling for an update on how things are going. The shoot is pretty much over now, so the film crew here in Prague give each other a round of applause and begin to pack away their equipment.

Blue's work in the Czech Republic is done. "This,"

Simon pronounces, "will be our best ever video." And that, as they say, is a wrap.

REHEARSING THE TOUR: PART TWO

chapter seven

WE'RE BACK IN THE south London rehearsal rooms. It's a few days since the lads were sat around with bits of paper on the table and they reckon they've got their set list together at last, though it's top secret so nobody's allowed to see it.

Blue have broken for lunch, and as they pick through a plate of sandwiches talk turns not to the imminent tour, which will be seen by 300,000 fans, but to the first ever live dates the band played together. It might not be a surprise to learn that the shows were hardly glamorous.

Duncan reminisces about the under-18 nightclubs, the disco appearances, the school gigs and the university tours. "I'll be honest with you," he begins. "In the early days that's how we earned our money as Blue. We'd go out, during the 'All Rise' period, and we'd do gigs for a pittance. I remember one of the gigs we did really early on in Birmingham, there wasn't even a stage! We were right there in the middle of the dancefloor and they just formed a circle around us. There were fifty people there with their arms folded, thinking, 'What on earth are these people doing in front of us.' But at the end of the day the money we made got split between us. Which in those days was amazing – that was our bread and butter. Anyway, it's not just about money – each show was another bit of publicity for us – it all helped to raise our profile."

Ant remembers those shows fondly. They were sometimes shambolic but they were always a laugh, and they were a great way for the band to learn their craft. "I'd love to go back and do them once again because for me that was one of the best times of being in Blue," he reveals. "We were just learning *all the time*.

It's like an apprentice footballer: he has to start at the bottom, he has to clean the professionals' boots until he gets that chance. We did get bottles thrown at us on stage, but that makes you a good band; that makes you stronger."

Lee, who hasn't found a sandwich to his liking but is making do with a packet of crisps, isn't worried about the size of an audience. "I could perform to ten people or ten thousand people," he says. "As long as I'm performing to someone we feel we have a place. Am I an exhibitionist? Yes, I think I probably am, but we vibe off each other on stage, we mess around, we don't know what we're gonna do next and it's a really relaxed atmosphere. It's not really about 'Look at me, I'm Lee Ryan', it's more of a collective thing where we're working as a band."

With the tour imminent, it also means that the boys can look forward to slipping into their old on-the-road routines. It's a prospect they relish, since it means they'll be back with their tour 'family' – the dancers, musicians and the other vital parts of the crew who make a Blue tour tick along. And as Simon points out, there's no room for ego in the Blue family. "Last year we spoke to the band and the dancers, we got everyone together and we said, 'Look, there's one thing we want you to know – this is a one-bus tour. We don't want to be separated from you lot."

Most bands, when they're on tour, will insist that they have their own tourbus, and that the 'less impor-tant' crew members must travel separately. "The dancers were looking at us all strange," Simon laughs, "as if to say 'Are you all right in the head?' It was like they'd never been treated like this before. I was like, 'Well if it wasn't for you we wouldn't look so good on stage, and you're not going to be giving great perform-ances every night if you're not happy, so get your stuff on our bus!' Thing is, we're gonna remember this tour for the rest of our lives, and we want to remember it for the right reasons."

Of course, back in the early days sharing a tourbus

wasn't even an option – conditions were cramped and the boys even had to share hotel rooms to keep costs down. "I'm all for sharing," Simon says, "but when you're with someone 24 hours a day it can get a bit much, so I think we're all happy now we've got our own hotel rooms on the road."

Living in such close proximity for such a long period of time, privacy is a real luxury. "It's hard," Antony explains. "Sometimes I like to make the lads laugh and I think that's what I was brought on this earth to do, just to make people laugh. But then sometimes you just have bad days, and you just want to keep yourself quiet. It works differently every day. One of us might be tired, one of us might want to chill out and go to sleep for a couple of hours. It doesn't mean we're not mates; we've spent nearly three years together and if we're a bit huffy every now and again it's not like we're never going to speak to each other ever again. But we know now that if someone's having a bad day, you leave them to get on with it. There's a real sense of understanding you get on the road – a real bond which is difficult to explain."

At this point Simon adds that Lee doesn't seem to have got the hang of the separate rooms concept – often he'll barge into Simon's room, run into the bathroom, do something horrendous in the toilet and then run off again. "I think it's just a habit," Simon muses. "I don't think he can poo in his own toilet. I used to have that in my friend's house. Every day, I used to go to my friend's house, and poo, and he used to be like 'Why do you always come to my house for a crap? Why don't you poo in your own house?' I'm like, 'I don't know, man.'"

So far today the boys have been running through the choreography for four songs – 'All Rise', 'One Love', 'Fly By' and 'If You Come Back', all of whose moves have progressed from the last time those songs were performed live.

"The thing about Blue," Simon explains, "is that when we have a routine, someone will always mess it up at some point. It's funny! Sometimes you'll see bands live and you see the band having a go at each other going, 'Your finger's in the wrong place! You're not putting your heart into this group, blah blah blah,' and whenever I see that happen I just think it's such a shame – if something's the same every night it gets boring for the band and therefore boring for the audience. If we mess up, we just laugh at each other."

Going back to the set list dilemma, the boys reveal that the running order, supposedly a 'secret', hasn't actually yet been finalised. "Obviously, we'll go through the ones that are really energetic," Simon says, "but there's a lot of vibey tracks on the second album that we didn't perform last time round which we really want to try and get into this tour. There'll be songs that everyone knows, because I think everyone who's coming out to see us will have those first two albums by now, and what we'll probably do is throw in some of the new material somewhere in the middle."

"Plus," Ant interrupts, "we're not going to be just

throwing ballads into the set for the sake of catching our breath and getting a few lighters in the air. For us, a ballad for us has to be a good ballad." He pauses to think for a while. "Fortunately, we've got quite a few of those!"

And in case you're wondering: the boys *have* decided to include encores in their set list, even though the concept of planning them seems a little ironic. Surely everyone knows the band haven't played their most popular songs – so why pretend you've gone off stage?

Simon laughs. "Well," he smiles, "we'd like to change that but it's just tradition, innit? You have to do an encore when you're on tour. It wouldn't be right otherwise – people would be still standing there for 20 minutes just looking up, going, 'Er, are they coming out again or what?' You know yourself when you go and see your favourite band that you'll have to wait until the end to hear the big hits. But that's a good lesson in being patient, I think."

Although the boys are all looking forward to being

out on the road and having a laugh, one thing they all agree on is the fact that the *biggest* buzz of being on tour comes from meeting fans all around the country – and they're a varied old lot.

"We've always thought our fans are slightly different from your average pop band," Ant says, "and when we've been out on the road – especially on the last arena tour – that's really proved us right. But it's interesting how fans differ around the country." In Belfast, he says, the audience were quite young, while Newcastle's crowd were up their in their early 20s. "We get all sorts. Mums, dads, uncles, aunts, kids, grandmas, grand-dads… It's fantastic to look out into the audience and see all those different faces looking back."

The boys are also keen to stress how strongly they feel about the importance of fans getting value for money when they come to see a live performance. The costs of making a live show truly spectacular have to be recouped through ticket sales – and the boys know that this means a number of their fans digging deep into their pocket money. It is, each of the boys admits, quite a lot of responsibility.

"We understand that it's not cheap going to a gig," Duncan says, nodding. "The face value of a ticket can just a be a starting point as sometimes fans need to stay overnight as well. We understand that fans are placing a high value on seeing our show and we want to make sure that their expectation is repaid. We want our fans to leave a show feeling that it's worth more than money to have that experience. To us that means there's no option not to make an effort. We give the best performance we can, every single night of the tour."

Lee knows exactly what Duncan's getting at. "It's not just about going through the motions on stage," he states, "we truly enjoy and take pride in our perform-ances. It's all about entertaining the audience."

Swinging on the back legs of his chair in a manner banned throughout the schools of Great Britain, Ant agrees. "We want to satisfy our fans, it's not fair to just deliver a second rate show. We believe in giving a quality live performance. This year, as last year, we've got a live band and we're going to use that band to its full potential. We've even got two more dancers on board for this year's show."

Lunch is now finished and the boys must get back to work. There's more rehearsing to be done, more dance moves to be learned, and more set list debates to be settled. Over the past few months we've seen these boys in a variety of situations and now, watching them train for the biggest tour of their career, they look like they're on a total high. Performing in front of their fans clearly means a lot to them and right now they're focused on delivering the best shows possible.

Antony grabs his microphone and makes his way over to the stage. "I know it's a cliché," he begins. "And I know we always say it. But if it wasn't for our fans we'd be nowhere, and the thought of getting out there again and seeing them all is just..." His voice trails away. It's an emotional moment and he just can't find the words.

Simon watches Ant take his position on the stage

next to Duncan and Lee. The band are ready to rehearse their opening number.

"Man," he eventually says. "I can't wait."

BLUE's third studio album

'Guilty', with 15 brand new

tracks including the hit single

'Guilty' and 'Signed, Sealed,

Delivered I'm Yours' featuring

Stevie Wonder & Angie Stone

hits the stores 3rd November.

Other **BLUE** titles also available from Contender Books

Blue on Blue HB £14.99
ISBN 1843570262

Blue on Blue PB £7.99
ISBN 1843570882

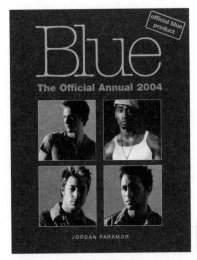

Blue Annual 2004 £5.99
ISBN 1843570734

blue

Official Blue Fan Club Membership

Our Fan Club belongs to Duncan and Antony's mums and is run with love by a very friendly team. OBFC has grown substantially in the last two years and has earned a reputation for being one of the best fan clubs around.

Becoming a member is simpler than ever! We have an automated online system, accepting all major credit cards and cheque payments, as well as our fan club HOTLINE. If you don't own a PC or would simply like to write to us, you can send in a SAE and we will send you back a printed joining form. All our details can be found below:

Write to us at:

OBFC – Official Blue Fan Club
PO Box 5329, Wimborne BH21 4XN

Telephone your order on: 01202 598738 (Mon-Fri 8.45am-6.00pm)
Or join online: join@officialbluefanclub.com

We invite you to visit our wicked funky website:

www.officialbluefanclub.com

We now proudly offer you the choice from 3 exciting membership levels:

Official Membership: £10 per year

- Exclusive Official Blue Fan Club, interactive multimedia CD (as standard) worth £12.99. (Or funky shiny black OBFC bag if you do not have a computer)
- Your own personal OBFC Membership ID number
- 10% discount on all Official Blue Fan Club Merchandise
- Exclusive access to Members' Area – includes message board, newsletters, selected venue ticket allocations, updates on gigs and much more.
- As a member we will put your very own photos of Blue up in our funky photo Gallery if you desire.
- Quarterly funky OBFC Newsletter

Social Membership: £17.50 per year

- Social membership offers everything that the Official membership offers plus exclusive access to OBFCChat.
- OBFCChat is an exclusive 3D Blue chat house, which allows you to chat in real time to other OBFC members. You can choose and customise your own characters, chat in the safety of this 3D secure environment and play games too it's a must see! Totally wicked! View the online demo at www.officialbluefanclub.com/obfchat/demo

VIP Membership: £25 per year

- This is our top of the range, exclusive membership, which includes all the benefits that the above memberships have to offer plus your very own BLUEmail account
- BLUEmail is your very own personalised Blue email, a great alternative to IloveBlue@somethingorother.com and others alike
- BLUEmail allows you to choose your very own email address from one of our OBFC domains (9 to choose from)
- Access to your emails from any computer connected to the Internet – great for staying in touch while on holiday
- A large 10MB of email storage (more available)

We also help out the boys with their mail, which we pass on to them at regular meetings. Find out more about these membership types at www.officialbluefanclub.com/register

NB. If you are purchasing from outside the UK, paying by foreign cheque or Euros, please add £5 to your order for bank transaction charges